CONSTITUTION -I
Student's Hand Book on The Constitution of India

Dr. Shyamali Mukherjee Bhattacharya

Assistant Professor of Law

Surendranath Law College, Kolkata

Preface

"India serves us the best by the Constitution,

Now it's our turn to serve it best as a Citizen"

As a teacher with over 16 years of experience in the field of Law, it has been my privilege to witness firsthand the transformative power of understanding the foundational principles that govern our societies. Throughout my career, I have strived to instill in my students a deep appreciation for the Constitution, not merely as a legal document, the bedrock of our democratic ideals and the guarantor of our rights and freedoms, but a value book for everyone.

This book, born out of years of teaching, discussions, and reflections, aims to serve as a comprehensive guide for students embarking on their journey through the intricacies of Constitution Law. It is designed to be a companion that simplifies complex concepts, elucidates historical contexts, and invites critical analysis of judicial interpretations and legislative evolution.

The study of constitutional principles is not merely an academic pursuit; it is a vital exercise in understanding the very essence of our governance and our responsibilities as citizens. With this in mind, this book endeavours to present the Constitution not as a static text, but as a living document that evolves with our society's changing needs and aspirations.

Finally, I invite you, the reader, to embark on this intellectual journey with an open mind and a readiness to explore the complexities and nuances of Constitution Law. May this book serve as a guiding light as you navigate through the profound concepts that define our legal framework.

Acknowledgements

Writing this book on Constitution Law has been a labour of love, shaped by the support and encouragement of many whom I am privileged to acknowledge.

First and foremost, I express my deepest gratitude to the Almighty God for granting me the passion, perseverance, and inspiration to undertake this endeavour.

To my parents and my mother in law whose love, sacrifices, and unwavering belief in my abilities have been the bedrock of my journey in education and beyond, I owe a debt of gratitude beyond words.

To my father-in-law, whose wisdom and encouragement have been a constant source of strength, thank you for your unwavering support.

I am indebted to my PhD supervisor, philosopher and Guide Prof.(Dr.) P.K.Sarkar, whose guidance, expertise, and mentorship laid the foundation for my career in academia and legal scholarship. Your insights continue to shape my approach to teaching and writing.

To my teachers, whose dedication to imparting knowledge and nurturing intellectual curiosity has profoundly influenced my own teaching philosophy, thank you for your invaluable contributions.

I extend my heartfelt thanks to my colleagues, past and fellow educators, whose insights and scholarly discussions have broadened my perspective and enriched the content of this book. Your collaboration has been invaluable.

I am grateful to my spouse, whose meticulous editing and feedback contributed significantly to the clarity and coherence of the manuscript. Your support, attention to detail and thoughtful suggestions have been immensely appreciated.

Finally, to my daughter and family for their patience, understanding, and love throughout this journey, I extend my deepest gratitude.

Dr. Shyamali Mukherjee Bhatttacharya

SYLLABUS

UNIVERSITY OF CALCUTTA

B.A.LL.B. (5-years Course)

SEMESTER-IV

Paper -- III

Constitutional Law -I

1. The Preamble: its importance and utility.
2. Fundamental Rights.
3. Directive Principles: its relation with fundamental rights
4. Fundamental duties.

Books Recommended:

I. Durga Das Basu - Constitutional Law of India.
2. Durga Das Basu — Shorter Constitution of India.
3. Durga Das Basu - Case book on Indian Constitution.
4. V. N. Sukla — Constitution of India.
5. H.P. Jain - Indian Constitutional Law.
6. M. Hidayatullah -- Constitutional Law of India.
7. T.K. Tope -- Constitutional Law of India.
8. J.N. Pande -- Constitutional law of India.
9. H.K. Saha Ray -- Constitution of India.
10. I. Bhatt — Fundamental Rights.

Table of Content

Chapter-I
The Constitution of India: Overview..15

Introduction 15
Historical Background 15
Constituent Assembly 16
Structure of the Constitution 16
Parts and Articles in Constitution 17
Schedules 23
Key Features and Principles 24
Landmark Amendments 25
Conclusion 26

Chapter II
The Preamble: Its Importance and Utility 27

Introduction 27
Text of the Preamble 27
Importance of the Preamble 28
Nature of the Indian State 28
Objectives of the Constitution 29

Utility of the Preamble 29
Judicial Interpretation of the Preamble 31
Conclusion 33

Chapter –III(i)
Structural Overview: Fundamental Rights under the Constitution of India 34

Introduction 34
Historical Background 34
Classification of Fundamental Rights 34
Significance of Fundamental Rights 37
Judicial Interpretation and Expansion 38
Limitations and Restrictions 39
Conclusion 39

Chapter-III(ii)
Fundamental Rights 41
The Right to Equality 41

Key Takeaways for Students 41
Introduction 42
Historical Context and Philosophical Foundations 42
Overview of Articles 14 to 18 42
Conceptual 43
Doctrine of Reasonable Classification 43

Practical Application 45

Challenges and Criticisms 46

Article 15: Prohibition of Discrimination on Grounds of Religion, Race, Caste, Sex, or Place of Birth 47

Article 16: Equality of Opportunity in Matters of Public Employment 48

Article 17: Abolition of Untouchability 48

Article 18: Abolition of Titles 48

Judicial Interpretation and Landmark Cases 49

Comparative Perspective 50

Challenges and Contemporary Issues 50

Conclusion 51

Chapter-III(iii)(A) Fundamental Rights to Freedom 52

Key Takeaways for Students 52

Introduction 52

Historical Context and Philosophical Foundations 53

Overview of Articles 19 to 22 53

Reasonable Restrictions 54

Article 20: Protection in Respect of Conviction for Offenses 54

Significance of Fundamental Rights to Freedom 55

Judicial Interpretation and Landmark Cases 56

Comparative Perspective 57

Challenges and Contemporary Issues 57

Conclusion 58

Chapter-III(iii)B
Fundamental Right to Life & Personal Liberty: Article 21......59

Introduction 59
Historical Context 59
Scope and Interpretation 60
Judicial Interpretation of Article 21 60
Expansion of Scope 60
Key Aspects of Article 21 60
Conclusion 63

Chapter-III(iii) C
Protection against Arrest and Detention: Article 22..................65

Introduction 65
Historical Context 65
Structure of Article 22 65
Judicial Interpretation 67
Preventive Detention Laws 68

Chapter-III (iv)
Fundamental Rights against Exploitation............................69

Key Takeaways for Students 69

Introduction 69

Historical Context and Philosophical Foundations 70

Overview of Articles 23 and 24 70

Significance of Fundamental Rights against Exploitation 71

Judicial Interpretation and Landmark Cases 72

Comparative Perspective 73

Challenges and Contemporary Issues 73

Conclusion 74

Chapter III (v)
Fundamental Right to Freedom of Religion 75

Key Takeaways for Students 75

Introduction 75

Historical Context and Philosophical Foundations 76

Overview of Articles 25 to 28 76

Significance of the Right to Freedom of Religion 78

Judicial Interpretation and Landmark Cases 79

Comparative Perspective 79

Challenges and Contemporary Issues 80

Conclusion 80

Chapter-III (vi)
Fundamental Rights to Cultural and Educational Rights 82

Key Takeaways for Students 82

Introduction 82
Historical Context and Philosophical Foundations 83
Overview of Articles 29 and 30 83
Significance of Cultural and Educational Rights 84
Judicial Interpretation and Landmark Cases 85
Comparative Perspective 86
Challenges and Contemporary Issues 86
Conclusion 87

Chapter-III(vii)
Fundamental Right to Constitutional Remedies 88

Key Takeaways for Students 88
Introduction 88
Historical Context and Philosophical Foundations 89
Overview of Article 32 89
Types of Writs under Article 32 90
Significance of the Right to Constitutional Remedies 91
Judicial Interpretation and Landmark Cases 92
Comparative Perspective 92
Challenges and Contemporary Issues 93
Conclusion 93

Chapter-IV(i)
Directive Principles of State Policy 95

Historical Background and Philosophical Foundation 95

Objectives of Directive Principles 95

Key Provisions of the Directive Principles 96

Nature and Significance 98

Implementation and Challenges 98

Judicial Interpretation and Evolution 99

Conclusion 100

Chapter-IV(ii)
The Relationship between Directive Principles of State Policy and Fundamental Rights 101

Introduction 101

Fundamental Rights: An Overview 101

Directive Principles of State Policy: An Overview 102

Complementary Nature 103

Conflict and Judicial Interpretation 103

Reconciliatory Approach 104

Implementation and Legislative Measures 105

Comparative Chart: 105

Conclusion 110

Chapter-V
Fundamental Duties under the Constitution of India 111

Introduction 111
Historical Background 111
Nature and Scope 112
Significance of Fundamental Duties 112
List of Fundamental Duties 113
Analysing Fundamental Duties...114
Importance of Fundamental Duties 119
Fundamental Duties and Education 121
Judicial Interpretation and Enforcement 122
Comparative Perspective 124
Challenges in Implementation 124
Conclusion...125

CHAPTER-I

The Constitution of India: Over view

Introduction

The Constitution of India is the supreme law of the country, serving as the framework for political principles, procedures, and powers of government institutions. It delineates the structure, procedures, powers, and duties of government institutions and sets out fundamental rights, directive principles, and the duties of citizens. Dr. B.R. Ambedkar is often hailed as the principal architect of the Indian Constitution, which was adopted on 26th November 1949 and came into effect on 26th January 1950.

Historical Background

Colonial Rule and the Demand for Independence

India was under British colonial rule for nearly 200 years. The struggle for independence was marked by various movements, protests, and demands for self-governance. Key events that paved the way for the formation of the Indian Constitution include:

1. **1857 Rebellion**: Often referred to as the First War of Indian Independence, it was a major but unsuccessful uprising against the British East India Company's rule.
2. **Formation of the Indian National Congress (1885)**: The Congress played a pivotal role in the Indian independence movement, articulating Indian aspirations and demands for self-rule.

3. **Montagu-Chelmsford Reforms (1919)**: Introduced diarchy in provinces, where elected Indian representatives were given some measure of control over domestic affairs.
4. **Government of India Act (1935)**: This act provided for greater self-governance but fell short of granting full independence.
5. **Cripps Mission (1942)**: An attempt by the British government to secure Indian cooperation during World War II by promising eventual self-government.
6. **Quit India Movement (1942)**: A mass protest demanding an end to British rule, led by Mahatma Gandhi.

Constituent Assembly

The Constituent Assembly was formed in 1946 to draft the Constitution of India. It consisted of elected representatives from various provinces and princely states. Dr. Rajendra Prasad was elected as the President of the Constituent Assembly, and Dr. B.R. Ambedkar was appointed as the Chairman of the Drafting Committee.

The assembly debated over numerous sessions, considering various aspects of governance, rights, and federalism. The draft was prepared after extensive discussions, debates, and consultations, drawing from diverse sources and legal traditions.

Structure of the Constitution

The Constitution of India is one of the longest written constitutions in the world. It originally had 395 articles, 22 parts, and 8 schedules. As of now, it consists of 470 articles, divided into 25 parts, and 12 schedules due to subsequent amendments.

Preamble

The Preamble serves as the introduction to the Constitution, outlining the fundamental values and guiding principles. It states:

"We, the people of India, having solemnly resolved to constitute India into a Sovereign Socialist Secular Democratic Republic and to secure to all its citizens:

- Justice, social, economic and political;
- Liberty of thought, expression, belief, faith and worship;
- Equality of status and of opportunity; and to promote among them all
- Fraternity assuring the dignity of the individual and the unity and integrity of the Nation;

In our Constituent Assembly this twenty-sixth day of November, 1949, do hereby adopt, enact and give to ourselves this Constitution."

Parts and Articles in Constitution

Part I: The Union and its Territory

This part deals with the name and territory of India, stating that "India, that is Bharat, shall be a Union of States." It provides the legal framework for the formation of new states, alteration of areas, boundaries, or names of existing states.

Part II: Citizenship

Part II (Articles 5-11) lays down the provisions relating to citizenship at the commencement of the Constitution, acquisition and termination of citizenship, and the authority of the Parliament to regulate citizenship by law.

Part III: Fundamental Rights

Fundamental Rights (Articles 12-35) are a cornerstone of the Constitution, guaranteeing civil liberties to all citizens to ensure individual dignity and democratic functioning.

Part IV: Directive Principles of State Policy

Directive Principles (Articles 36-51) are guidelines for the government to frame policies and laws. These principles aim to establish social and economic democracy and are non-justiciable, meaning they cannot be enforced by the courts. Key principles include:

- Providing adequate means of livelihood.
- Ensuring equal pay for equal work.
- Protecting the environment.
- Promoting education and public health.

Part IVA: Fundamental Duties

Added by the 42nd Amendment in 1976, Part IVA (Article 51A) outlines the Fundamental Duties of citizens, emphasizing moral and civic responsibilities such as:

- Respecting the Constitution and national symbols.
- Promoting harmony and spirit of common brotherhood.
- Protecting the environment.
- Developing scientific temper and humanism.

Part V: The Union

Part V (Articles 52-151) deals with the executive, legislative, and judicial branches of the Union Government. Key articles include:

- **The President (Articles 52-62)**: Describes the election, powers, and duties of the President.
- **Parliament (Articles 79-122)**: Details the composition, powers, and procedures of the Parliament.
- **Union Judiciary (Articles 124-147)**: Establishes the Supreme Court and outlines its jurisdiction and powers.

Part VI: The States

Part VI (Articles 152-237) mirrors the provisions of Part V but pertains to State Governments. It includes:

- **The Governor (Articles 153-162)**: Describes the appointment, powers, and duties of Governors.
- **State Legislatures (Articles 168-212)**: Details the composition, powers, and procedures of state legislatures.
- **State Judiciary (Articles 214-237)**: Establishes High Courts and outlines their jurisdiction and powers.

Part VII: The States in Part B of the First Schedule

This part has been repealed by the 7th Amendment Act, 1956.

Part VIII: The Union Territories

Part VIII (Articles 239-242) deals with the administration of Union Territories, which are directly governed by the Union Government.

Part IX: The Panchayats

Added by the 73rd Amendment in 1992, Part IX (Articles 243-243O) institutionalizes Panchayati Raj, providing a framework for decentralized governance at the village level.

Part IXA: The Municipalities

Added by the 74th Amendment in 1992, Part IXA (Articles 243P-243ZG) provides for the establishment and governance of urban local bodies, promoting decentralized urban governance.

Part IXB: The Cooperative Societies

Added by the 97th Amendment in 2011, Part IXB (Articles 243ZH-243ZT) outlines the formation, regulation, and autonomy of cooperative societies.

Part X: The Scheduled and Tribal Areas

Part X (Articles 244-244A) contains special provisions for the administration and control of Scheduled and Tribal Areas, ensuring the protection and development of Scheduled Tribes.

Part XI: Relations between the Union and the States

Part XI (Articles 245-263) delineates the distribution of legislative, administrative, and executive powers between the Union and the States, emphasizing federalism.

Part XII: Finance, Property, Contracts, and Suits

Part XII (Articles 264-300A) deals with the financial relations between the Union and the States, including the distribution of revenue, property management, and the conduct of government contracts and suits.

Part XIII: Trade, Commerce, and Intercourse within the Territory of India

Part XIII (Articles 301-307) ensures the freedom of trade, commerce, and intercourse throughout the territory of India, promoting economic unity.

Part XIV: Services under the Union and the States

Part XIV (Articles 308-323) deals with the recruitment and conditions of service for persons serving under the Union and State Governments.

Part XIVA: Tribunals

Part XIVA (Articles 323A-323B) provides for the establishment of administrative and other tribunals to adjudicate disputes and complaints related to public services and other matters.

Part XV: Elections

Part XV (Articles 324-329A) deals with the conduct of elections to Parliament, State Legislatures, and the offices of the President and Vice-President. It establishes the Election Commission of India to supervise elections.

Part XVI: Special Provisions relating to certain classes

Part XVI (Articles 330-342) contains special provisions for the representation and upliftment of Scheduled Castes, Scheduled

Tribes, and other backward classes, ensuring their inclusion and protection.

Part XVII: Official Language

Part XVII (Articles 343-351) deals with the official language of the Union, regional languages, and the promotion and development of Hindi.

Part XVIII: Emergency Provisions

Part XVIII (Articles 352-360) contains provisions for dealing with emergencies, including national emergency, President's rule in states, and financial emergency.

Part XIX: Miscellaneous

Part XIX (Articles 361-367) contains miscellaneous provisions, including the protection of the President and Governors, the effect of failure to comply with certain directives, and the definition of key terms used in the Constitution.

Part XX: Amendment of the Constitution

Part XX (Article 368) outlines the procedure for amending the Constitution, requiring a special majority in Parliament and, in certain cases, ratification by at least half of the State Legislatures.

Part XXI: Temporary, Transitional and Special Provisions

Part XXI (Articles 369-392) contains temporary, transitional, and special provisions, including those related to the reorganization of states and the continuance of existing laws and their adaptation.

Part XXII: Short Title, Commencement, Authoritative Text in Hindi and Repeals

Part XXII (Articles 393-395) deals with the short title, commencement, authoritative text in Hindi, and the repeal of the Government of India Act, 1935, and other laws inconsistent with the Constitution.

Schedules

The Constitution originally had eight schedules, which have since increased to twelve:

1. **First Schedule**: Lists the states and union territories and their territorial jurisdictions.
2. **Second Schedule**: Deals with the emoluments, allowances, and privileges of the President, Governors, Judges, and other constitutional officeholders.
3. **Third Schedule**: Contains the forms of oaths and affirmations for various constitutional and statutory officeholders.
4. **Fourth Schedule**: Allocates seats for each state in the Rajya Sabha (Council of States).
5. **Fifth Schedule**: Contains provisions related to the administration and control of Scheduled Areas and Scheduled Tribes.
6. **Sixth Schedule**: Deals with the administration of tribal areas in the states of Assam, Meghalaya, Tripura, and Mizoram.
7. **Seventh Schedule**: Contains the Union List, State List, and Concurrent List, detailing the subjects on which the Union and State Governments can legislate.

8. **Eighth Schedule**: Lists the official languages recognized by the Constitution.
9. **Ninth Schedule**: Contains laws that are exempt from judicial review, primarily to protect land reform and other socio-economic legislation.
10. **Tenth Schedule**: Contains provisions related to the disqualification of Members of Parliament and State Legislatures on the grounds of defection (Anti-Defection Law).
11. **Eleventh Schedule**: Lists the powers, authority, and responsibilities of Panchayats.
12. **Twelfth Schedule**: Lists the powers, authority, and responsibilities of Municipalities.

Key Features and Principles

Federal Structure with Unitary Bias

India follows a federal structure with a strong unitary bias, meaning there is a clear division of powers between the Union and the State Governments, but in certain circumstances, the Union Government holds overriding authority. This ensures a balance between unity and regional autonomy.

Parliamentary System of Government

India adopts the parliamentary system of government, where the executive is responsible to the legislature. The President is the nominal executive head, while the Prime Minister and the Council of Ministers are the real executive authorities.

Secularism

The Constitution declares India to be a secular state, meaning there is no state religion. It ensures that all religions are treated equally and prohibits discrimination on the grounds of religion.

Socialism

The term "socialist" was added to the Preamble by the 42nd Amendment, reflecting the commitment to social justice, aiming to reduce inequalities in income and eliminate exploitation in all forms.

Fundamental Rights and Duties

The Constitution guarantees fundamental rights to all citizens, ensuring civil liberties, and imposes fundamental duties on citizens, promoting a sense of responsibility and national pride.

Judicial Independence

The judiciary in India is independent, ensuring the impartiality and fairness of judicial proceedings. The Supreme Court is the highest judicial authority, followed by High Courts at the state level and subordinate courts.

Amendment Procedure

The Constitution provides a flexible yet rigorous amendment procedure, allowing for necessary changes while preserving the fundamental framework. Amendments require a special majority in Parliament and, in certain cases, ratification by state legislatures.

Landmark Amendments

The Constitution of India has undergone several amendments to address emerging needs and challenges. Some landmark amendments include:

1. **First Amendment (1951)**: Addressed issues related to land reform and added restrictions to the right to freedom of speech.
2. **Seventh Amendment (1956)**: Reorganized states on linguistic lines.
3. **Twenty-fourth Amendment (1971)**: Affirmed the Parliament's power to amend any part of the Constitution.
4. **Forty-second Amendment (1976)**: Known as the "Mini-Constitution," it made extensive changes, including the addition of Fundamental Duties and changes to the Preamble.
5. **Forty-fourth Amendment (1978)**: Restored the balance of power between the executive and the judiciary and reinstated civil liberties curtailed during the Emergency.
6. **Seventy-third and Seventy-fourth Amendments (1992)**: Strengthened local self-government by institutionalizing Panchayati Raj and urban local bodies.

Conclusion

The Constitution of India is a living document that has evolved over time to meet the aspirations and challenges of a diverse and dynamic society. It reflects the core values of democracy, justice, liberty, equality, and fraternity, guiding the nation towards inclusive and sustainable development. For students, understanding the Constitution is crucial not only for academic purposes but also for becoming informed and responsible citizens who contribute to the nations progress and uphold its democratic ideals.

CHAPTER- II

The Preamble: Its Importance and Utility

Introduction

The Preamble to the Constitution of India is much more than a mere introduction to the document. It encapsulates the essence, philosophy, and objectives of the Constitution. Drafted with profound insight and wisdom, the Preamble reflects the vision of the framers and serves as a guiding light for the interpretation of the Constitution. For students of constitutional law, understanding the Preamble is crucial as it lays the foundation for comprehending the broader principles enshrined in the Constitution.

Text of the Preamble

"We, the people of India, having solemnly resolved to constitute India into a Sovereign Socialist Secular Democratic Republic and to secure to all its citizens:

- Justice, social, economic and political;
- Liberty of thought, expression, belief, faith and worship;
- Equality of status and of opportunity; and to promote among them all
- Fraternity assuring the dignity of the individual and the unity and integrity of the Nation;

In our Constituent Assembly this twenty-sixth day of November, 1949, do hereby adopt, enact and give to ourselves this Constitution."

Importance of the Preamble

Source of Authority

The Preamble begins with the words "We, the people of India," signifying that the ultimate authority of the Constitution rests with the people of India. This concept of popular sovereignty emphasizes that the Constitution is created by and for the people, reflecting their collective will and aspirations.

Nature of the Indian State

The Preamble declares India to be a "Sovereign Socialist Secular Democratic Republic." Each of these terms carries significant weight:

- Sovereign: India is an independent nation, free from external control. It has the power to make its own laws and policies.
- Socialist: Emphasizing social and economic equality, the term reflects the aim to eliminate inequalities in income, status, and standards of living.
- Secular: The state does not uphold any religion as the official religion, ensuring that all religions are treated equally and there is no religious discrimination.
- Democratic: India follows a system of representative democracy, where the government is elected by the people, ensuring political equality and participation.

- Republic: The head of the state is elected and not a hereditary monarch, reinforcing the principles of equality and democratic governance.

Objectives of the Constitution

The Preamble outlines the core objectives of the Constitution, which are:

- Justice: The Preamble ensures justice in social, economic, and political aspects. This means creating a fair and equitable society, providing equal opportunities for all, and protecting the rights of citizens.
- Liberty: It guarantees the freedom of thought, expression, belief, faith, and worship. These freedoms are essential for the development of individuals and the functioning of a democratic society.
- Equality: The Preamble promises equality of status and opportunity, aiming to eliminate discrimination and provide equal chances for all to progress.
- Fraternity: Promoting a sense of brotherhood, the Preamble assures the dignity of the individual and the unity and integrity of the nation. It underscores the importance of national unity and solidarity.

Utility of the Preamble

Interpretative Tool

The Preamble serves as a key to understanding the intentions of the framers of the Constitution. When the language of the Constitution is ambiguous, courts often refer to the Preamble to interpret its provisions. It acts as a guiding star, illuminating the objectives and guiding principles that the Constitution seeks to achieve.

Reflection of Aspirations

The Preamble reflects the aspirations of the people of India. It captures the vision of an inclusive, just, and equitable society. For students, it provides a glimpse into the ideals that the framers envisioned for the nation. Understanding these aspirations helps students appreciate the broader goals of the Constitution and the legal framework it establishes.

Foundation of Constitutional Values

The values enshrined in the Preamble form the bedrock of the Constitution. These values guide the interpretation and application of the Constitution, ensuring that laws and policies align with the fundamental principles of justice, liberty, equality, and fraternity. For students, these values provide a moral and ethical foundation for studying and understanding constitutional law.

Guiding Governance and Policy Making

The objectives stated in the Preamble guide the functioning of the government and the formulation of policies. Governments are expected to frame laws and policies that uphold justice, promote liberty, ensure equality, and foster fraternity. For students aspiring to work in public policy or governance, the Preamble serves as a blueprint for creating a just and equitable society.

Inspiration for Social Change

The Preamble inspires social change by emphasizing justice, equality, and fraternity. It serves as a reminder of the collective responsibility to build a society where every individual is treated with dignity and respect. For students, the Preamble is a call to action, encouraging them to contribute to the nation's progress and uphold its democratic ideals.

Role in Constitutional Amendments

The Preamble has also played a crucial role in the context of constitutional amendments. The 42nd Amendment Act (1976) added the words "Socialist" and "Secular" to the Preamble, reflecting the evolving aspirations of the nation. This amendment underscored the dynamic nature of the Constitution and the significance of the Preamble in adapting to changing societal values.

Judicial Interpretation of the Preamble

Historic Judgments

The Preamble has been the subject of interpretation in various landmark judgments by the Supreme Court of India. These judgments highlight the significance of the Preamble in constitutional interpretation and its role in shaping the legal landscape.

Kesavananda Bharati Case (1973)

In the landmark case of Kesavananda Bharati v. State of Kerala (1973), the Supreme Court held that the Preamble is an integral part of the Constitution. The court asserted that the Preamble embodies the basic structure of the Constitution, which cannot be altered by any amendment. This judgment established the doctrine of the basic structure, ensuring that certain fundamental principles of the Constitution remain inviolable.

Berubari Union Case (1960)

In the Berubari Union Case (1960), the Supreme Court observed that the Preamble is not a source of power or limitations but serves as a guiding principle for interpreting the Constitution. The court emphasized that the Preamble reflects the intentions and aspirations of the framers and should be used to understand the true spirit of the Constitution.

S.R. Bommai Case (1994)

In the S.R. Bommai v. Union of India (1994) case, the Supreme Court reiterated the significance of the Preamble in interpreting the Constitution. The court emphasized the secular nature of the Indian state, as declared in the Preamble, and held that any action undermining secularism would be unconstitutional. This judgment reinforced the importance of the Preamble in safeguarding the core values of the Constitution.

Conclusion

The Preamble to the Constitution of India is a powerful and profound statement of the nation's fundamental values and objectives. It encapsulates the essence of the Constitution, reflecting the vision and aspirations of the framers. For students, understanding the Preamble is essential as it provides the foundation for comprehending the broader principles and values enshrined in the Constitution.

The Preamble's importance lies in its role as a source of authority, a reflection of the nation's ideals, and a guiding tool for interpreting the Constitution. Its utility extends to shaping governance, inspiring social change, and providing a moral and ethical framework for constitutional law.

As students delve deeper into the study of the Constitution, the Preamble serves as a beacon, illuminating the path towards a just, equitable, and inclusive society. By embracing the values enshrined in the Preamble, students can contribute to the realization of the constitutional vision and uphold the democratic ideals that define the nation.

CHAPTER-III

Structural Overview: Fundamental Rights under the Constitution of India

Introduction

Fundamental Rights are the cornerstone of the Indian Constitution, guaranteeing essential freedoms and liberties to every citizen. Enshrined in Part III of the Constitution, these rights are designed to protect individuals from arbitrary state action and to promote equality, freedom, and justice. This chapter provides a detailed exploration of the Fundamental Rights, their significance, scope, and judicial interpretation, offering students a comprehensive understanding of their importance in the Indian constitutional framework.

Historical Background

The concept of Fundamental Rights in India draws inspiration from various sources, including the United States Bill of Rights, the British Constitution, and the Universal Declaration of Human Rights. During the drafting of the Indian Constitution, the framers, led by Dr. B.R. Ambedkar, emphasized the inclusion of Fundamental Rights to safeguard individual liberties and ensure justice and equality in an independent India.

Classification of Fundamental Rights

The Fundamental Rights are classified into six broad categories:

1. Right to Equality (Articles 14-18)

2. Right to Freedom (Articles 19-22)
3. Right against Exploitation (Articles 23-24)
4. Right to Freedom of Religion (Articles 25-28)
5. Cultural and Educational Rights (Articles 29-30)
6. Right to Constitutional Remedies (Article 32)

Each category encompasses specific rights that are crucial for the protection and promotion of individual liberties.

Right to Equality (Articles 14-18)

- Article 14: Ensures equality before the law and equal protection of the laws, prohibiting discrimination by the state.
- Article 15: Prohibits discrimination on grounds of religion, race, caste, sex, or place of birth.
- Article 16: Guarantees equality of opportunity in matters of public employment.
- Article 17: Abolishes untouchability and forbids its practice in any form.
- Article 18: Abolishes titles except military and academic distinctions.

Right to Freedom (Articles 19-22)

- Article 19: Guarantees six fundamental freedoms:
- Freedom of speech and expression
- Freedom to assemble peacefully without arms
- Freedom to form associations or unions
- Freedom to move freely throughout the territory of India
- Freedom to reside and settle in any part of India

Freedom to practice any profession or to carry on any occupation, trade, or business

- Article 20: Protects individuals in respect of conviction for offenses:
    - No ex-post facto law
    - No double jeopardy
    - No self-incrimination
- Article 21: Protects life and personal liberty, stating that no person shall be deprived of his life or personal liberty except according to the procedure established by law.
- Article 21A: Provides for free and compulsory education for children aged 6 to 14 years.
- Article 22: Provides protection against arrest and detention in certain cases, ensuring specific rights to individuals detained under ordinary law or preventive detention laws.

Right against Exploitation (Articles 23-24)

- Article 23: Prohibits traffic in human beings and forced labor.
- Article 24: Prohibits the employment of children below the age of 14 years in factories, mines, and other hazardous occupations.

Right to Freedom of Religion (Articles 25-28)

- Article 25: Guarantees freedom of conscience and the right to freely profess, practice, and propagate religion.
- Article 26: Guarantees the right to manage religious affairs.
- Article 27: Prohibits the state from compelling any person to pay taxes for the promotion of any particular religion.
- Article 28: Provides freedom as to attendance at religious instruction or religious worship in certain educational institutions.

Cultural and Educational Rights (Articles 29-30)

- Article 29: Protects the interests of minorities by providing them the right to conserve their culture, language, and script.
- Article 30: Guarantees minorities the right to establish and administer educational institutions of their choice.

Right to Constitutional Remedies (Article 32)

- Article 32: Empowers individuals to approach the Supreme Court for the enforcement of Fundamental Rights. This right to constitutional remedies is itself a Fundamental Right, and Dr. Ambedkar described it as the "heart and soul" of the Constitution.

Significance of Fundamental Rights

Fundamental Rights are essential for the following reasons:

1. Protection of Individual Liberty: They safeguard the personal freedoms of individuals against arbitrary state action.
2. Promotion of Equality: They ensure equal treatment of all citizens and prohibit discrimination.
3. Foundation of Democracy: They provide a framework for a democratic society by guaranteeing political freedoms and participation.
4. Socio-economic Justice: They aim to achieve social and economic justice by abolishing practices such as untouchability and child labor.
5. Judicial Enforcement: They empower individuals to seek judicial redress for the violation of their rights, ensuring accountability and rule of law.

Judicial Interpretation and Expansion

The judiciary, particularly the Supreme Court, has played a pivotal role in interpreting and expanding the scope of Fundamental Rights. Some landmark judgments include:

- Kesavananda Bharati v. State of Kerala (1973): Introduced the basic structure doctrine, asserting that the fundamental framework of the Constitution cannot be altered by amendments.
- Maneka Gandhi v. Union of India (1978): Expanded the interpretation of Article 21 to include the right to a fair and reasonable procedure, thus broadening the scope of personal liberty.
- Vishaka v. State of Rajasthan (1997): Recognized sexual harassment at the workplace as a violation of gender equality and the right to life and personal liberty under Articles 14, 15, and 21.
- Navtej Singh Johar v. Union of India (2018): Decriminalized consensual homosexual acts between adults, affirming the rights to equality, privacy, and non-discrimination.

Limitations and Restrictions

While Fundamental Rights are paramount, they are not absolute and are subject to reasonable restrictions in the interest of:

- Security of the State
- Public Order
- Decency or Morality
- Contempt of Court
- Defamation
- Incitement to an Offense

- Sovereignty and Integrity of India

These restrictions ensure a balance between individual freedoms and the collective interests of society.

Conclusion

Fundamental Rights are the bedrock of the Indian Constitution, ensuring the protection of individual liberties, promoting equality, and fostering a democratic society. Understanding these rights, their scope, and their judicial interpretation is crucial for students to appreciate the role of the Constitution in safeguarding democracy and justice in India. Through continuous judicial interpretation and societal commitment, Fundamental Rights continue to evolve, reflecting the dynamic nature of the Indian constitutional framework.

CHAPTER-III(ii)

Fundamental Rights

The Right to Equality

Key Takeaways for Students

- Understand the Scope: Familiarize yourself with the specific provisions of Articles 14 to 18 and their significance.
- Analyze Judicial Interpretation: Study landmark judgments to understand how the judiciary has interpreted and expanded the Right to Equality.
- Appreciate the Challenges: Recognize the contemporary issues and challenges in achieving substantive equality in India.
- Comparative Analysis: Compare the Right to Equality in India with similar provisions in other constitutions to gain a broader perspective.

By grasping these concepts, students can develop a comprehensive understanding of the Right to Equality and its pivotal role in the Indian constitutional framework.

Introduction

The Right to Equality is a cornerstone of the Indian Constitution, enshrined in Articles 14 to 18 of Part III. These provisions aim to abolish social inequalities and ensure equal treatment for all citizens. As students of constitutional law, understanding the Right to Equality is crucial, as it forms the foundation of a just and equitable society. This chapter explores the scope, significance, and judicial interpretations of the Right to Equality in India.

Historical Context and Philosophical Foundations

The framers of the Indian Constitution were deeply influenced by the principles of equality and non-discrimination, drawing inspiration from various international documents and constitutions, such as the Universal Declaration of Human Rights and the United States Constitution. The Right to Equality in India seeks to eliminate the historical injustices and social inequalities prevalent in Indian society.

Overview of Articles 14 to 18

Article 14: Equality before Law and Equal Protection of the Laws

- Scope: Article 14 guarantees that the state shall not deny to any person equality before the law or the equal protection of the laws within the territory of India.
- Principle: It embodies the concept of equality as a dynamic principle, allowing for reasonable classification but prohibiting arbitrary discrimination.
- Judicial Interpretation: In the case of *State of West Bengal v. Anwar Ali Sarkar*, the Supreme Court held that while classification is permissible, it must be reasonable and not arbitrary.

Conceptual Framework

1. Equality before Law:

Article 14 of the Indian Constitution enshrines the principle of equality before the law and equal protection of the laws within the territory of India. This provision forms the bedrock of the doctrine of reasonable classification. Equality before the law implies the absence of any special privilege by reason of birth, creed, or the like and emphasizes equal subjection to all persons to the ordinary law of the land.

2. Equal Protection of Laws:

The concept of equal protection of laws, borrowed from the 14th Amendment of the U.S. Constitution, goes beyond mere formal equality. It mandates substantive equality by requiring the state to treat equally all persons who are similarly circumstanced. However, it does not imply that all laws must apply universally to all individuals.

Doctrine of Reasonable Classification

The doctrine of reasonable classification is a cornerstone of constitutional law, ensuring that the law treats individuals equitably while permitting necessary distinctions. Rooted in the principles of equality and non-discrimination, reasonable classification ensures that any differentiation made by the law is justifiable, serving a legitimate state interest without being arbitrary or discriminatory.

1. Basis of Classification:

The doctrine of reasonable classification allows the state to classify individuals into groups and treat them differently, provided the classification meets two primary criteria:

- Intelligible Differentia: The classification must be based on an intelligible differentia, distinguishing persons or things grouped together from others left out of the group.
- Rational Nexus: There must be a rational nexus between the basis of classification and the objective sought to be achieved by the law.

2. Judicial Interpretation:

The judiciary has played a pivotal role in elucidating the principles of reasonable classification. The landmark case of *State of West Bengal v. Anwar Ali Sarkar* laid down the foundation for this doctrine. Subsequently, in *E.P. Royappa v. State of Tamil Nadu*, the Supreme Court expanded the understanding of equality, emphasizing that equality is a dynamic concept with many aspects and dimensions.

3. Tests of Valid Classification:

In *State of Kerala v. N.M. Thomas*, the Supreme Court established a test to determine the reasonableness of classification:

- The classification must not be arbitrary, artificial, or evasive.
- There must be a substantial basis for the differentiation.
- The object of classification should be lawful and must not defeat the constitutional mandate of equality.

Practical Application

1. Affirmative Action:

Reasonable classification justifies affirmative action policies, such as reservations in education and employment for Scheduled Castes, Scheduled Tribes, and Other Backward Classes. The Supreme Court, in *Indra Sawhney v. Union of India*, upheld the constitutionality of reservations, emphasizing that affirmative action serves the purpose of achieving substantive equality.

2. Taxation Laws:

Taxation laws often employ reasonable classification to impose different tax rates on different categories of persons or activities. The rationale is to achieve economic objectives and ensure progressive taxation, as seen in *Kunnathat Thathunni Moopil Nair v. State of Kerala*.

3. Gender-Based Laws:

Gender-based classification, if justified by an intelligible differentia and rational nexus, is permissible. In *Air India v. Nargesh Meerza*, the Supreme Court struck down discriminatory service conditions for air hostesses but acknowledged that certain gender-specific provisions could be valid if they serve a legitimate state interest.

Challenges and Criticisms

1. Arbitrary Classifications:

One of the significant challenges is the potential for arbitrary or discriminatory classifications. Laws that fail to meet the criteria of intelligible differentia and rational nexus are liable to be struck down as unconstitutional, as seen in *D.S. Nakara v. Union of India*.

2. Evolving Standards:

The standards of reasonable classification evolve with societal changes. What may be considered reasonable at one time may not hold the same status later, necessitating continuous judicial scrutiny and reinterpretation.

3. Balancing Interests:

Balancing individual rights and state interests is an intricate task. The judiciary must carefully scrutinize the purpose and impact of classifications to ensure they align with constitutional values.

The doctrine of reasonable classification ensures that while the law can differentiate between individuals and groups, such differentiation must be justified by an intelligible differentia and a rational nexus to the objective sought. This doctrine is pivotal in maintaining a balance between individual equality and societal needs, reflecting the dynamic nature of constitutional law. By understanding and applying these principles, legal practitioners and scholars can better appreciate the intricate balance between equality and classification in the pursuit of justice.

Article 15: Prohibition of Discrimination on Grounds of Religion, Race, Caste, Sex, or Place of Birth

- Scope: Article 15 prohibits discrimination by the state on the grounds of religion, race, caste, sex, or place of birth.
- Positive Discrimination: It allows for special provisions for women and children, and for the advancement of

socially and educationally backward classes, Scheduled Castes, and Scheduled Tribes.
- Judicial Interpretation: In *Navtej Singh Johar v. Union of India*, the Supreme Court held that Article 15(1) includes protection against discrimination based on sexual orientation.

Article 16: Equality of Opportunity in Matters of Public Employment

- Scope: Article 16 guarantees equality of opportunity for all citizens in matters relating to employment or appointment to any office under the state.
- Reservations: It permits the state to make reservations for any backward class of citizens that, in the opinion of the state, is not adequately represented in public services.
- Judicial Interpretation: In the landmark case of *Indra Sawhney v. Union of India* (Mandal Commission case), the Supreme Court upheld the principle of reservations but imposed a ceiling of 50% on the total reservations.

Article 17: Abolition of Untouchability

- Scope: Article 17 abolishes "untouchability" and forbids its practice in any form.
- Legislation: The Protection of Civil Rights Act, 1955, was enacted to enforce Article 17 and prescribe punishments for the practice of untouchability.
- Judicial Interpretation: The judiciary has consistently upheld the provisions of Article 17, emphasizing the eradication of untouchability as a fundamental goal.

Article 18: Abolition of Titles

- Scope: Article 18 prohibits the state from conferring any titles, except military or academic distinctions, and prevents Indian citizens from accepting titles from any foreign state.
- Rationale: The abolition of titles aims to establish a classless society and prevent the creation of artificial distinctions among people.
- Judicial Interpretation: The Supreme Court in *Balaji Raghavan v. Union of India* clarified that national awards like Bharat Ratna and Padma Vibhushan are not "titles" within the meaning of Article 18.

Judicial Interpretation and Landmark Cases

The judiciary has played a pivotal role in interpreting and expanding the scope of the Right to Equality. Some landmark judgments include:

1. State of West Bengal v. Anwar Ali Sarkar (1952): This case dealt with the principle of reasonable classification under Article 14. The Supreme Court held that any classification must be based on intelligible differentia and must have a rational relation to the object sought to be achieved.
2. E.P. Royappa v. State of Tamil Nadu (1974): The Supreme Court introduced the concept of equality as a dynamic principle, emphasizing that equality is antithetical to arbitrariness. This case marked a significant shift in the judicial approach towards Article 14.
3. Maneka Gandhi v. Union of India (1978): The Supreme Court expanded the interpretation of Article 21 and linked it with Article 14, stating that the procedure

established by law must be "right, just and fair," thereby incorporating the principle of equality into the right to personal liberty.
4. Indra Sawhney v. Union of India (1992): The Mandal Commission case dealt with reservations in public employment under Article 16. The Supreme Court upheld the principle of reservations for backward classes but imposed a 50% ceiling on the total reservations to maintain the balance between equality and affirmative action.
5. Navtej Singh Johar v. Union of India (2018): In this landmark case, the Supreme Court decriminalized consensual homosexual acts between adults, affirming the rights to equality and non-discrimination under Articles 14 and 15.

Comparative Perspective

The Right to Equality in India can be compared with similar provisions in other constitutions, such as the Equal Protection Clause in the United States Constitution and the Equality Act in the United Kingdom. These comparisons highlight both similarities and unique features of the Indian approach to equality.

Challenges and Contemporary Issues

Despite the constitutional guarantees, achieving substantive equality remains a challenge in India. Issues such as caste discrimination, gender inequality, and socio-economic disparities continue to persist. The judiciary and legislature must work together to address these challenges and ensure the effective realization of the Right to Equality.

Conclusion

The Right to Equality is fundamental to the Indian Constitution's vision of a just and equitable society. Understanding the scope, significance, and judicial interpretation of Articles 14 to 18 is crucial for students of constitutional law. As future legal practitioners and scholars, it is essential to recognize the role of the Right to Equality in promoting social justice and ensuring the dignity of all individuals in India.

CHAPTER-III(iii)(A)

Fundamental Rights to Freedom

Key Takeaways for Students

- **Understand the Scope**: Familiarize yourself with the specific provisions of Articles 19 to 22 and their significance.
- **Analyze Judicial Interpretation**: Study landmark judgments to understand how the judiciary has interpreted and expanded these rights.
- **Appreciate the Challenges**: Recognize the contemporary issues and challenges in achieving the full realization of Fundamental Rights to Freedom.
- **Comparative Analysis**: Compare these rights with similar provisions in other constitutions to gain a broader perspective.

By grasping these concepts, students can develop a comprehensive understanding of the Fundamental Rights to Freedom and their pivotal role in the Indian constitutional framework.

Introduction

The Fundamental Rights to Freedom enshrined in Part III of the Indian Constitution form the bedrock of individual liberty and democracy. These rights, articulated in Articles 19 to 22, ensure that citizens can express themselves, move freely, and enjoy personal liberties, subject to reasonable restrictions. This chapter provides an in-depth exploration of these rights, their scope, significance, and judicial interpretation, offering students a comprehensive understanding of their importance in the Indian constitutional framework.

Historical Context and Philosophical Foundations

The inclusion of Fundamental Rights to Freedom in the Indian Constitution reflects the framers' commitment to individual liberty and democratic principles. Influenced by the Bill of Rights in the United States Constitution and the Universal Declaration of Human Rights, the framers sought to protect citizens from arbitrary state actions and to promote a free and democratic society.

Overview of Articles 19 to 22

Article 19: Protection of Certain Rights Regarding Freedom of Speech, etc.

Article 19 guarantees six fundamental freedoms to all citizens:

1. **Freedom of Speech and Expression**: Allows citizens to express their opinions freely without fear of retribution.
2. **Freedom to Assemble Peacefully**: Grants the right to hold meetings and demonstrations, provided they are peaceful and unarmed.
3. **Freedom to Form Associations or Unions**: Ensures the right to form and join groups, societies, or trade unions.
4. **Freedom to Move Freely Throughout the Territory of India**: Allows citizens to travel and reside in any part of the country.

5. **Freedom to Reside and Settle in Any Part of India**: Permits citizens to choose their place of residence and settlement within the country.
6. **Freedom to Practice Any Profession, or to Carry on Any Occupation, Trade, or Business**: Guarantees the right to choose one's occupation and engage in any trade or business.

Reasonable Restrictions: Each of these freedoms is subject to reasonable restrictions in the interests of sovereignty and integrity of India, security of the state, public order, decency or morality, contempt of court, defamation, and incitement to an offense.

Article 20: Protection in Respect of Conviction for Offenses

Article 20 provides three important protections to individuals in case of criminal offenses:

1. **No Ex-Post Facto Law**: No person shall be convicted for an act that was not an offense at the time it was committed.
2. **No Double Jeopardy**: No person shall be prosecuted and punished for the same offense more than once.
3. **No Self-Incrimination**: No person accused of an offense shall be compelled to be a witness against himself.

Article 21: Protection of Life and Personal Liberty

Article 21 states that no person shall be deprived of his life or personal liberty except according to the procedure established by law. This article has been expansively interpreted by the judiciary to include a wide range of rights.

Article 21A: Right to Education

Article 21A, added by the 86th Amendment Act of 2002, provides for free and compulsory education to all children aged 6 to 14 years.

Article 22: Protection Against Arrest and Detention in Certain Cases

Article 22 provides specific protections to individuals against arbitrary arrest and detention:

1. **Right to be Informed of Grounds of Arrest**: Any person arrested must be informed of the reasons for the arrest.
2. **Right to Consult and Be Defended by a Legal Practitioner**: The arrested person has the right to consult and be represented by a lawyer of their choice.
3. **Right to be Produced Before a Magistrate within 24 Hours**: The arrested person must be presented before a magistrate within 24 hours of arrest, excluding travel time.
4. **Protection Against Preventive Detention**: Specific safeguards are provided for individuals detained under preventive detention laws.

Significance of Fundamental Rights to Freedom

The Fundamental Rights to Freedom are essential for the following reasons:

1. **Promotion of Democracy**: These rights ensure that citizens can participate freely in the democratic process.
2. **Protection of Individual Liberty**: They safeguard personal freedoms and protect individuals from arbitrary state actions.
3. **Encouragement of Free Expression**: They promote a culture of open dialogue and dissent, which is vital for a vibrant democracy.
4. **Economic Freedom**: By guaranteeing the freedom to practice any profession or trade, they support economic liberty and entrepreneurship.

Judicial Interpretation and Landmark Cases

The judiciary has played a critical role in interpreting and expanding the scope of Fundamental Rights to Freedom. Some landmark judgments include:

1. **Maneka Gandhi v. Union of India (1978)**: The Supreme Court expanded the interpretation of Article 21 to include the right to a fair and reasonable procedure, thus broadening the scope of personal liberty.
2. **A.K. Gopalan v. State of Madras (1950)**: The Supreme Court initially took a narrow view of Article 21, but this interpretation was later expanded in subsequent cases.
3. **Shreya Singhal v. Union of India (2015)**: The Supreme Court struck down Section 66A of the Information Technology Act, which criminalized online speech, as unconstitutional, affirming the right to free speech under Article 19(1)(a).
4. **Vishaka v. State of Rajasthan (1997)**: The Supreme Court laid down guidelines to prevent sexual harassment

at the workplace, linking the right to a safe working environment with Articles 19 and 21.
5. **Navtej Singh Johar v. Union of India (2018)**: The Supreme Court decriminalized consensual homosexual acts between adults, affirming the rights to equality, privacy, and non-discrimination.

Comparative Perspective

Comparing the Fundamental Rights to Freedom in India with similar provisions in other democratic constitutions, such as the First Amendment of the United States Constitution and the European Convention on Human Rights, reveals both similarities and unique features. For example:

- **Freedom of Speech**: While both the Indian and U.S. Constitutions guarantee freedom of speech, the reasonable restrictions in India provide a different framework for balancing individual rights with societal interests.
- **Right to Life and Personal Liberty**: The expansive interpretation of Article 21 in India, encompassing a wide range of rights such as the right to privacy and the right to a clean environment, demonstrates the dynamic nature of judicial interpretation.

Challenges and Contemporary Issues

Despite the constitutional guarantees, achieving full realization of Fundamental Rights to Freedom faces several challenges:

1. **Censorship and Free Speech**: Balancing free speech with reasonable restrictions remains a contentious issue, particularly in the digital age.

2. **Preventive Detention**: The use of preventive detention laws has raised concerns about the potential for abuse and violation of personal liberties.
3. **Right to Privacy**: With advancements in technology, protecting the right to privacy has become increasingly complex.
4. **Economic Barriers**: Ensuring equal access to opportunities and addressing socio-economic disparities is essential for the full realization of economic freedoms.

Conclusion

The Fundamental Rights to Freedom are integral to the Indian Constitution's vision of a democratic and just society. Understanding the scope, significance, and judicial interpretation of Articles 19 to 22 is crucial for students of constitutional law. As future legal practitioners and scholars, it is essential to recognize the role of these rights in promoting individual liberty and democratic principles in India.

CHAPTER-III(iii)B

Fundamental Right to Life & Personal Liberty: Article 21

Introduction

Article 21 of the Indian Constitution is one of the most crucial and dynamic provisions safeguarding the fundamental rights of individuals. It succinctly states, "No person shall be deprived of his life or personal liberty except according to procedure established by law." Despite its brevity, Article 21 has been expansively interpreted by the judiciary to encompass a wide array of rights essential to human dignity. This chapter delves into the various aspects of Article 21, including its historical context, scope, judicial interpretations, and landmark case laws.

Historical Context

The inclusion of Article 21 in the Indian Constitution was inspired by similar provisions in other democratic constitutions, particularly the Due Process Clause of the United States Constitution. However, the framers chose the phrase "procedure established by law" over "due process of law" to limit judicial overreach. Initially, Article 21 was interpreted narrowly, but over time, judicial activism has significantly broadened its scope.

"No person shall be deprived of his life or personal liberty except according to procedure established by law."

This provision ensures that any deprivation of life or personal liberty must follow a procedure that is lawful, fair, and reasonable.

Scope and Interpretation

The scope of Article 21 has been expanded through various landmark judgments by the Supreme Court of India, transforming it from a mere procedural right to a fountainhead of several substantive rights.

Judicial Interpretation of Article 21

1. **A.K. Gopalan v. State of Madras (1950)**: The Supreme Court initially adopted a narrow interpretation, holding that "procedure established by law" meant any procedure prescribed by a validly enacted law, irrespective of its fairness or reasonableness.

Expansion of Scope

2. **Maneka Gandhi v. Union of India (1978)**: This landmark case marked a paradigm shift. The Supreme Court ruled that the "procedure established by law" must be fair, just, and reasonable. It linked Article 21 with Article 14 (Right to Equality) and Article 19 (Right to Freedom), establishing that laws infringing on personal liberty must pass the tests of reasonableness and non-arbitrariness.

Key Aspects of Article 21

Right to Life

The right to life under Article 21 is not merely a physical right but includes the right to live with human dignity and all that goes along with it.

1. **Francis Coralie Mullin v. Administrator, Union Territory of Delhi (1981)**: The Supreme Court held that the right to life includes the right to live with human dignity, nutrition, clothing, shelter, and the right to carry on activities that constitute the bare necessities of life.
2. **Olga Tellis v. Bombay Municipal Corporation (1985)**: The Court recognized the right to livelihood as an integral part of the right to life.

Right to Personal Liberty

Personal liberty encompasses a variety of rights, protecting individuals from arbitrary state actions.

1. **Kharak Singh v. State of Uttar Pradesh (1964)**: The Court held that unauthorized intrusion into a person's home violated personal liberty.
2. **Satwant Singh Sawhney v. D. Ramarathnam (1967)**: It was held that the right to travel abroad is part of personal liberty under Article 21.

Right to Privacy

The right to privacy has emerged as a crucial facet of Article 21 through judicial interpretation.

1. **K.S. Puttaswamy v. Union of India (2017)**: In a landmark judgment, the Supreme Court unanimously recognized the right to privacy as a fundamental right under Article 21. This judgment has far-reaching implications for data protection, surveillance, and personal autonomy.

Right to Health

The right to health has been recognized as an essential part of the right to life.

1. **Parmanand Katara v. Union of India (1989)**: The Supreme Court held that the state has an obligation to preserve life and directed that no medical authority shall refuse immediate medical treatment to a person in need.
2. **Paschim Banga Khet Mazdoor Samity v. State of West Bengal (1996)**: The Court emphasized that providing adequate medical facilities is an obligation of the government and is an integral part of the right to life.

Right to Education

The right to education has been linked with the right to life.

1. **Mohini Jain v. State of Karnataka (1992)**: The Supreme Court held that the right to education at all levels is a fundamental right under Article 21.
2. **Unni Krishnan v. State of Andhra Pradesh (1993)**: The Court clarified that the right to education is implicit in the right to life and personal liberty, mandating the state to provide educational facilities to all children up to the age of 14 years.

Right to a Clean Environment

The right to a clean and healthy air, water, environment has been recognized as part of the right to life.

1. **Subhash Kumar v. State of Bihar (1991)**: The Supreme Court acknowledged that the right to life

includes the right to enjoyment of pollution-free air and water.

Right Against Inhuman Treatment

Article 21 has been interpreted to prohibit inhuman and degrading treatment.

1. **D.K. Basu v. State of West Bengal (1997)**: The Supreme Court laid down detailed guidelines to prevent custodial violence and deaths, reinforcing the right against torture and inhuman treatment.

Right to Fair Trial

The right to a fair trial is an essential part of personal liberty under Article 21.

1. **Hussainara Khatoon v. Home Secretary, State of Bihar (1979)**: The Supreme Court highlighted the right to a speedy trial as an essential part of Article 21.
2. **Niharendu Dutt Majumdar v. Emperor (1942)**: The right to free legal aid was recognized as part of the right to a fair trial under Article 21.

Conclusion

Article 21 of the Indian Constitution, through judicial interpretation, has evolved into a bedrock of numerous substantive rights essential for human dignity and liberty. The expansive interpretation by the judiciary has ensured that Article 21 remains a dynamic and living provision, capable of addressing contemporary challenges and protecting individual rights against arbitrary state actions.

Chapter-III(iii) C

Protection against Arrest and Detention: Article 22

Introduction

Article 22 of the Indian Constitution is a significant provision that safeguards the rights of individuals against arbitrary arrest and detention. Embedded in the framework of fundamental rights, Article 22 provides both preventive and punitive measures to ensure that the state does not misuse its power to detain individuals.

Historical Context

The genesis of Article 22 can be traced back to the colonial era, where the arbitrary use of power by the British government led to widespread discontent. The framers of the Indian Constitution, drawing lessons from this period, sought to create a legal safeguard against similar abuses in independent India. The debates in the Constituent Assembly reflect a conscious effort to balance state security with individual liberty.

Structure of Article 22

Article 22 is structured into two main parts:

1. **Clause (1) and (2): Protections against Arrest and Detention**
    - Clause (1) ensures that no person who is arrested shall be detained in custody without being

informed, as soon as may be, of the grounds for such arrest, and shall have the right to consult and be defended by a legal practitioner of their choice.
- Clause (2) mandates that the person arrested must be produced before the nearest magistrate within 24 hours of arrest, excluding the time necessary for the journey from the place of arrest to the court, and no person shall be detained beyond this period without the authority of a magistrate.

2. **Clauses (3) to (7): Preventive Detention**
    - Clause (3) provides an exception for preventive detention laws, where the rights conferred by Clauses (1) and (2) are not applicable.
    - Clause (4) requires that no law providing for preventive detention shall authorize the detention of a person for a period exceeding three months unless an Advisory Board reports sufficient cause for the continued detention.
    - Clause (5) ensures that the person detained under preventive detention laws is informed of the grounds of detention and is afforded the earliest opportunity to make a representation against the order.
    - Clause (6) allows the state to withhold facts from disclosure if it is against public interest.
    - Clause (7) empowers the Parliament to prescribe the maximum period for which a person can be detained under any law providing for preventive detention and the procedure to be followed by the Advisory Board.

Judicial Interpretation

Over the years, the Indian judiciary has played a pivotal role in interpreting Article 22, balancing individual rights with the state's power to ensure national security and public order.

Landmark Judgments

1. **A.K. Gopalan v. State of Madras (1950)**
   - This case was one of the earliest to interpret Article 22, where the Supreme Court upheld the preventive detention laws, emphasizing that Article 22 is self-contained and independent of Article 21.

2. **Maneka Gandhi v. Union of India (1978)**
   - A significant shift occurred with this case, where the Supreme Court expanded the scope of Article 21 and held that any law depriving a person of their life or personal liberty must be just, fair, and reasonable, thereby indirectly influencing the interpretation of Article 22.

3. **ADM Jabalpur v. Shivkant Shukla (1976)**
   - During the Emergency period, the Supreme Court's controversial decision stated that even the right to life could be suspended, reflecting the tension between state power and individual rights. However, this was later overruled, reinforcing the judiciary's commitment to protecting fundamental rights.

Practical Implications

Article 22 has profound implications for the legal and constitutional framework in India. It provides a crucial check on the executive's power to detain individuals and ensures that such power is exercised within the bounds of legality and fairness.

Preventive Detention Laws

Various preventive detention laws in India, such as the National Security Act (NSA) and the Conservation of Foreign Exchange and Prevention of Smuggling Activities Act (COFEPOSA), operate within the framework provided by Article 22. These laws have been subject to scrutiny and challenges to ensure they do not undermine the fundamental rights guaranteed by the Constitution.

Article 22 of the Indian Constitution embodies a delicate balance between individual liberty and state security. Its provisions are a testament to the framers' foresight in safeguarding against the misuse of state power while allowing for necessary measures to maintain public order and national security. Understanding the historical context, judicial interpretations, and practical applications of Article 22 is crucial for comprehending the broader framework of fundamental rights in India.

CHAPTER-III (iv)

Fundamental Rights against Exploitation

Key Takeaways for Students

- **Understand the Scope**: Familiarize yourself with the specific provisions of Articles 23 and 24 and their significance.
- **Analyze Judicial Interpretation**: Study landmark judgments to understand how the judiciary has interpreted and expanded these rights.
- **Appreciate the Challenges**: Recognize the contemporary issues and challenges in achieving the full realization of Fundamental Rights against Exploitation.
- **Comparative Analysis**: Compare these rights with similar provisions in other constitutions and international conventions to gain a broader perspective.

By grasping these concepts, students can develop a comprehensive understanding of the Fundamental Rights against Exploitation and their pivotal role in the Indian constitutional framework.

Introduction

The Fundamental Rights against Exploitation, enshrined in Articles 23 and 24 of Part III of the Indian Constitution, are critical to protecting human dignity and eliminating oppressive practices. These rights aim to eradicate practices such as human trafficking, forced labor, and child labor, which have long plagued Indian society. This chapter provides a detailed examination of these rights, their scope, significance, and judicial interpretation, offering students a comprehensive understanding of their importance in the Indian constitutional framework.

Historical Context and Philosophical Foundations

The inclusion of Fundamental Rights against Exploitation in the Indian Constitution reflects the framers' commitment to human dignity, social justice, and equality. Influenced by international conventions and a deep awareness of historical injustices, the framers sought to protect vulnerable populations from exploitation and to promote a just and humane society.

Overview of Articles 23 and 24

Article 23: Prohibition of Traffic in Human Beings and Forced Labor

- **Scope**: Article 23 prohibits trafficking in human beings, begar (forced labor), and other similar forms of forced labor. The term "traffic in human beings" includes the practice of selling and buying human beings like commodities, especially women and children.
- **Positive Measures**: The state can enact laws to provide for compulsory services for public purposes (such as conscription), provided such services are not discriminatory on the grounds of religion, race, caste, or class.
- **Judicial Interpretation**: In the landmark case of *People's Union for Democratic Rights v. Union of India* (1982), also known as the Asiad Workers' Case, the Supreme Court held that any labor without payment of

the minimum wage amounts to "forced labor" and is prohibited under Article 23.

Article 24: Prohibition of Employment of Children in Factories, etc.

- **Scope**: Article 24 prohibits the employment of children below the age of 14 years in factories, mines, or any other hazardous employment. This provision is aimed at protecting children from exploitation and ensuring their right to education and development.
- **Legislation**: The Child Labour (Prohibition and Regulation) Act, 1986, and subsequent amendments provide a legal framework for the enforcement of Article 24.
- **Judicial Interpretation**: In the case of *M.C. Mehta v. State of Tamil Nadu* (1996), the Supreme Court directed the government to take measures to ensure that children are not employed in hazardous industries and to rehabilitate children employed in such industries.

Significance of Fundamental Rights against Exploitation

The Fundamental Rights against Exploitation are essential for several reasons:

1. **Protection of Human Dignity**: They safeguard individuals from practices that demean human dignity and violate basic human rights.
2. **Promotion of Social Justice**: They aim to eliminate oppressive practices and promote a more equitable and just society.

3. **Protection of Vulnerable Populations**: They provide legal safeguards for vulnerable groups such as children, women, and economically disadvantaged individuals.
4. **Support for Economic Development**: By prohibiting forced labor and child labor, these rights promote fair labor practices and contribute to the overall economic development of the country.

Judicial Interpretation and Landmark Cases

The judiciary has played a crucial role in interpreting and enforcing the Fundamental Rights against Exploitation. Some landmark judgments include:

1. **People's Union for Democratic Rights v. Union of India (1982)**: The Supreme Court held that the non-payment of minimum wages amounts to forced labor under Article 23. This case expanded the understanding of forced labor and emphasized the need for just and humane working conditions.
2. **Bandhua Mukti Morcha v. Union of India (1984)**: The Supreme Court addressed the issue of bonded labor and directed the government to take steps for the identification, release, and rehabilitation of bonded laborers.
3. **M.C. Mehta v. State of Tamil Nadu (1996)**: The Supreme Court issued comprehensive guidelines for the elimination of child labor in hazardous industries and directed the establishment of welfare funds for the education and rehabilitation of children.
4. **Vishal Jeet v. Union of India (1990)**: The Supreme Court issued directives to curb child prostitution and trafficking, emphasizing the need for stringent enforcement of laws and the rehabilitation of victims.

Comparative Perspective

Comparing the Fundamental Rights against Exploitation in India with similar provisions in other constitutions and international conventions, such as the International Labour Organization (ILO) conventions and the United Nations Convention on the Rights of the Child (UNCRC), highlights both similarities and unique features of the Indian approach:

- **International Conventions**: India is a signatory to several ILO conventions and the UNCRC, which set global standards for the protection of children and workers from exploitation.
- **National Legislation**: The Indian legal framework, including the Bonded Labour System (Abolition) Act, 1976, and the Child Labour (Prohibition and Regulation) Act, 1986, reflects the country's commitment to eliminating exploitation and aligns with international standards.

Challenges and Contemporary Issues

Despite constitutional guarantees and legislative measures, several challenges persist in fully realizing the Fundamental Rights against Exploitation:

1. **Implementation and Enforcement**: Effective implementation and enforcement of laws remain a significant challenge due to lack of resources, corruption, and inadequate monitoring mechanisms.
2. **Socio-Economic Factors**: Poverty, illiteracy, and lack of access to education and employment opportunities contribute to the persistence of exploitative practices such as child labor and bonded labor.

3. **Awareness and Advocacy**: Increasing public awareness and advocacy efforts are essential to address the root causes of exploitation and to promote the rights and well-being of vulnerable populations.

Conclusion

The Fundamental Rights against Exploitation are integral to the Indian Constitution's vision of a just and humane society. Understanding the scope, significance, and judicial interpretation of Articles 23 and 24 is crucial for students of constitutional law. As future legal practitioners and scholars, it is essential to recognize the role of these rights in promoting human dignity, social justice, and equality in India.

Chapter III-v

Fundamental Right to Freedom of Religion

Key Takeaways for Students

- **Understand the Scope**: Familiarize yourself with the specific provisions of Articles 25 to 28 and their significance.
- **Analyze Judicial Interpretation**: Study landmark judgments to understand how the judiciary has interpreted and expanded these rights.
- **Appreciate the Challenges**: Recognize the contemporary issues and challenges in achieving the full realization of the right to freedom of religion.
- **Comparative Analysis**: Compare these rights with similar provisions in other constitutions to gain a broader perspective.

By grasping these concepts, students can develop a comprehensive understanding of the right to freedom of religion and its pivotal role in the Indian constitutional framework.

Introduction

The Fundamental Right to Freedom of Religion, enshrined in Articles 25 to 28 of Part III of the Indian Constitution, ensures that every individual has the right to profess, practice, and propagate their religion. This right reflects India's commitment to secularism, pluralism, and tolerance in a diverse society. This chapter delves into the scope, significance, and judicial interpretation of the right to freedom of religion, providing with a comprehensive understanding of its role and importance in the Indian constitutional framework.

Historical Context and Philosophical Foundations

The inclusion of the right to freedom of religion in the Indian Constitution was influenced by India's historical commitment to religious diversity and tolerance. The framers of the Constitution were deeply aware of the religious plurality in India and sought to protect individuals' rights to religious freedom while maintaining public order and societal harmony. They were also influenced by international documents like the Universal Declaration of Human Rights.

Overview of Articles 25 to 28

Article 25: Freedom of Conscience and Free Profession, Practice, and Propagation of Religion

- **Scope**: Article 25 guarantees to every individual the freedom of conscience and the right to freely profess, practice, and propagate religion, subject to public order, morality, and health.
- **State Interference**: The state can regulate or restrict any economic, financial, political, or other secular activities associated with religious practice and can provide for social welfare and reform.
- **Judicial Interpretation**: In *Shirur Mutt Case* (1954), the Supreme Court held that religious practices are protected under Article 25, but activities not essential to religion can be regulated by the state.

Article 26: Freedom to Manage Religious Affairs

- **Scope**: Article 26 grants every religious denomination or any section thereof the right to:
    1. Establish and maintain institutions for religious and charitable purposes.
    2. Manage its own affairs in matters of religion.
    3. Own and acquire movable and immovable property.
    4. Administer such property in accordance with the law.
- **Judicial Interpretation**: In *Sri Venkataramana Devaru v. State of Mysore* (1958), the Supreme Court clarified that while religious denominations have the autonomy to manage their affairs, they are subject to regulations for maintaining public order and morality.

Article 27: Freedom as to Payment of Taxes for Promotion of Any Particular Religion

- **Scope**: Article 27 ensures that no person shall be compelled to pay any taxes, the proceeds of which are specifically appropriated for the promotion or maintenance of any particular religion or religious denomination.
- **Judicial Interpretation**: In *T.M.A. Pai Foundation v. State of Karnataka* (2002), the Supreme Court reiterated that state funds should not be used to promote or sustain any particular religion.

Article 28: Freedom as to Attendance at Religious Instruction or Religious Worship in Certain Educational Institutions

- **Scope**: Article 28 provides for the following:
    1. No religious instruction shall be provided in any educational institution wholly maintained out of state funds.
    2. Religious instruction is permitted in educational institutions administered by the state but established under any endowment or trust requiring such instruction.
    3. No person attending any educational institution recognized by the state or receiving aid from state funds shall be required to participate in religious instruction or worship without their consent, or if a minor, without the consent of their guardian.
- **Judicial Interpretation**: The Supreme Court, in several cases, has upheld the principle of secular education and the protection of individual rights to choose participation in religious activities.

Significance of the Right to Freedom of Religion

The right to freedom of religion is essential for several reasons:

1. **Promotion of Secularism**: It ensures that the state does not favor any religion, maintaining a secular character.
2. **Protection of Religious Pluralism**: It protects the rights of individuals and groups to practice diverse religions, promoting harmony in a pluralistic society.
3. **Safeguarding Individual Liberty**: It upholds the freedom of conscience and the individual's right to choose and change their religion.
4. **Facilitating Social Reform**: It allows the state to intervene in religious practices that are detrimental to social welfare and reform.

Judicial Interpretation and Landmark Cases

The judiciary has played a crucial role in interpreting the right to freedom of religion, balancing individual rights with public order and social welfare. Some landmark judgments include:

1. **Commissioner of Hindu Religious Endowments, Madras v. Sri Lakshmindra Thirtha Swamiar of Sri Shirur Mutt (1954)**: This case established that the state cannot interfere in the essential practices of a religion.
2. **S.R. Bommai v. Union of India (1994)**: The Supreme Court upheld the principle of secularism as a basic feature of the Constitution, asserting that the state must maintain neutrality in religious matters.
3. **Bijoe Emmanuel v. State of Kerala (1986)**: The Court held that the expulsion of children from school for refusing to sing the national anthem on religious grounds violated their right to freedom of religion.
4. **Indian Young Lawyers Association v. State of Kerala (2018)**: The Supreme Court allowed the entry of women of all ages into the Sabarimala temple, asserting that the practice of barring women was unconstitutional and violated their right to equality and religious freedom.

Comparative Perspective

Comparing the right to freedom of religion in India with similar provisions in other constitutions, such as the First Amendment of the United States Constitution and the European Convention on Human Rights, reveals both similarities and unique features:

- **United States**: The First Amendment guarantees the free exercise of religion and prohibits the establishment

of religion. The U.S. emphasizes a strict separation of church and state.
- **European Convention on Human Rights**: Article 9 guarantees the right to freedom of thought, conscience, and religion, subject to limitations necessary in a democratic society for public safety, order, health, or morals.

Challenges and Contemporary Issues

Despite constitutional guarantees, several challenges persist in fully realizing the right to freedom of religion:

1. **Communal Violence**: Instances of communal violence and religious intolerance pose significant challenges to religious freedom.
2. **State Interference**: Balancing state intervention in religious practices with respect for religious autonomy remains contentious.
3. **Conversion and Anti-Conversion Laws**: The regulation of religious conversions and the enactment of anti-conversion laws have raised concerns about their impact on religious freedom.
4. **Educational Institutions**: The role of religious instruction in state-funded and private educational institutions continues to be a debated issue.

Conclusion

The right to freedom of religion is fundamental to the Indian Constitution's vision of a secular and pluralistic society. Understanding the scope, significance, and judicial interpretation of Articles 25 to 28 is crucial for students of constitutional law. As future legal practitioners and scholars, it is essential to recognize the role of this right in promoting religious harmony, individual liberty, and social justice in India.

CHAPTER-III (vi)

Fundamental Rights to Cultural and Educational Rights

Key Takeaways for Students

- **Understand the Scope**: Familiarize yourself with the specific provisions of Articles 29 and 30 and their significance.
- **Analyze Judicial Interpretation**: Study landmark judgments to understand how the judiciary has interpreted and expanded these rights.
- **Appreciate the Challenges**: Recognize the contemporary issues and challenges in achieving the full realization of cultural and educational rights.
- **Comparative Analysis**: Compare these rights with similar provisions in other constitutions and international conventions to gain a broader perspective.

By grasping these concepts, students can develop a comprehensive understanding of the cultural and educational rights and their pivotal role in the Indian constitutional framework.

Introduction

The Fundamental Rights to Cultural and Educational Rights, enshrined in Articles 29 and 30 of Part III of the Indian Constitution, are designed to protect the cultural heritage of minorities and to ensure their right to establish and administer educational institutions. These rights reflect India's commitment to preserving its diverse cultural fabric and promoting equality in educational opportunities. This chapter provides a detailed examination of these rights, their scope, significance, and judicial interpretation, offering students a comprehensive understanding of their importance in the Indian constitutional framework.

Historical Context and Philosophical Foundations

The inclusion of cultural and educational rights in the Indian Constitution stems from the recognition of India's vast cultural diversity and the need to protect the rights of minorities. The framers of the Constitution were influenced by the principles of equality, non-discrimination, and the importance of preserving cultural identities in a pluralistic society.

Overview of Articles 29 and 30

Article 29: Protection of Interests of Minorities

- **Article 29(1)**: Any section of the citizens residing in the territory of India or any part thereof having a distinct language, script, or culture of its own shall have the right to conserve the same.
- **Article 29(2)**: No citizen shall be denied admission into any educational institution maintained by the State or receiving aid out of State funds on grounds only of religion, race, caste, language, or any of them.

Significance:

- **Cultural Preservation**: Article 29(1) aims to protect and preserve the unique cultural identities of various groups within India.

- **Non-Discrimination**: Article 29(2) ensures that no citizen is discriminated against in admission to state-funded educational institutions, promoting equal access to education.

Article 30: Right of Minorities to Establish and Administer Educational Institutions

- **Article 30(1)**: All minorities, whether based on religion or language, shall have the right to establish and administer educational institutions of their choice.
- **Article 30(2)**: The State shall not, in granting aid to educational institutions, discriminate against any educational institution on the ground that it is under the management of a minority, whether based on religion or language.

Significance:

- **Educational Autonomy**: Article 30(1) provides minorities the autonomy to establish and administer their own educational institutions, ensuring that they can preserve and promote their cultural and educational values.
- **State Support**: Article 30(2) mandates that state aid should be provided without discrimination, ensuring that minority educational institutions are treated equally with other institutions.

Significance of Cultural and Educational Rights

The cultural and educational rights are essential for several reasons:

1. **Promotion of Pluralism**: They ensure the preservation of India's cultural diversity and promote pluralism.
2. **Protection of Minority Rights**: They protect the rights of minorities to maintain their cultural and educational institutions, fostering an inclusive society.
3. **Non-Discrimination in Education**: They guarantee equal access to educational opportunities for all citizens, regardless of their religious or linguistic background.
4. **Cultural Identity**: They empower minority communities to preserve their cultural identity and heritage through education.

Judicial Interpretation and Landmark Cases

The judiciary has played a crucial role in interpreting and enforcing the cultural and educational rights. Some landmark judgments include:

1. **St. Xavier's College v. State of Gujarat (1974)**: The Supreme Court held that the right to administer educational institutions includes the right to disciplinary control, admission of students, and appointment of staff, but reasonable regulations can be imposed by the state.
2. **T.M.A. Pai Foundation v. State of Karnataka (2002)**: The Supreme Court clarified the extent of autonomy enjoyed by minority institutions, holding that while the state can impose reasonable regulations, it cannot interfere with the minority character of the institutions.
3. **P.A. Inamdar v. State of Maharashtra (2005)**: The Supreme Court held that unaided minority institutions have the right to admit students of their choice, but the

state can impose conditions for maintaining standards of education.
4. **Ahmedabad St. Xavier's College Society v. State of Gujarat (1974)**: The Court reaffirmed that the right to establish and administer educational institutions includes the right to choose the governing body and staff.

Comparative Perspective

Comparing the cultural and educational rights in India with similar provisions in other constitutions and international conventions, such as the United Nations Declaration on the Rights of Indigenous Peoples (UNDRIP) and the European Convention on Human Rights, reveals both similarities and unique features:

- **International Conventions**: UNDRIP and other international documents emphasize the rights of indigenous peoples and minorities to preserve their cultural heritage and establish their own educational systems.
- **National Legislation**: Countries like Canada and Australia have similar provisions protecting the rights of indigenous peoples and minority groups, reflecting a global commitment to cultural preservation and educational equality.

Challenges and Contemporary Issues

Despite constitutional guarantees, several challenges persist in fully realizing the cultural and educational rights:

1. **Implementation and Enforcement**: Effective implementation and enforcement of these rights remain a

challenge due to bureaucratic hurdles and lack of awareness.
2. **Balancing Autonomy and Regulation**: Balancing the autonomy of minority institutions with the need for regulatory oversight to ensure quality education is a contentious issue.
3. **Resource Allocation**: Ensuring adequate resources and support for minority educational institutions to function effectively is crucial.
4. **Social Integration**: Promoting social integration while preserving cultural identities poses a delicate challenge in a diverse society like India.

Conclusion

The cultural and educational rights are integral to the Indian Constitution's vision of an inclusive and pluralistic society. Understanding the scope, significance, and judicial interpretation of Articles 29 and 30 is crucial for students of constitutional law. As future legal practitioners and scholars, it is essential to recognize the role of these rights in promoting cultural diversity, educational equality, and minority protection in India.

CHAPTER-III(vii)

Fundamental Right to Constitutional Remedies

Key Takeaways for Students

- **Understand the Scope**: Familiarize yourself with the specific provisions of Article 32 and the types of writs available for the enforcement of fundamental rights.
- **Analyze Judicial Interpretation**: Study landmark judgments to understand how the judiciary has interpreted and expanded the right to constitutional remedies.
- **Appreciate the Challenges**: Recognize the contemporary issues and challenges in achieving the full realization of the right to constitutional remedies.
- **Comparative Analysis**: Compare this right with similar provisions in other constitutions and international conventions to gain a broader perspective.

By grasping these concepts, students can develop a comprehensive understanding of the right to constitutional remedies and its pivotal role in the Indian constitutional framework.

Introduction

The Fundamental Right to Constitutional Remedies, enshrined in Article 32 of Part III of the Indian Constitution, is considered the cornerstone of the Indian democratic framework. This right provides citizens with the mechanism to enforce their fundamental rights through the judiciary. Dr. B.R. Ambedkar famously referred to Article 32 as the "heart and soul" of the Constitution because it ensures the protection and enforcement of all other fundamental rights. This chapter delves into the scope, significance, and judicial interpretation of the right to constitutional remedies, offering students a comprehensive understanding of its crucial role in the Indian constitutional framework.

Historical Context and Philosophical Foundations

The inclusion of the right to constitutional remedies in the Indian Constitution was influenced by the need to provide effective legal recourse to individuals whose fundamental rights have been violated. The framers of the Constitution recognized that without the ability to enforce rights, the declaration of fundamental rights would be meaningless. They drew inspiration from various sources, including the American Bill of Rights and British common law, to ensure that citizens had access to justice through the courts.

Overview of Article 32

Article 32: Remedies for Enforcement of Rights Conferred by Part III

- **Article 32(1)**: The right to move the Supreme Court by appropriate proceedings for the enforcement of the rights conferred by this Part is guaranteed.
- **Article 32(2)**: The Supreme Court shall have power to issue directions or orders or writs, including writs in the nature of habeas corpus, mandamus, prohibition, quo warranto, and certiorari, whichever may be appropriate,

for the enforcement of any of the rights conferred by this Part.
- **Article 32(3)**: Without prejudice to the powers conferred on the Supreme Court by clauses (1) and (2), Parliament may by law empower any other court to exercise within the local limits of its jurisdiction all or any of the powers exercisable by the Supreme Court under clause (2).
- **Article 32(4)**: The right guaranteed by this article shall not be suspended except as otherwise provided for by this Constitution.

Article 32 provides for

- **Judicial Protection**: Article 32 provides individuals with direct access to the Supreme Court for the enforcement of fundamental rights.
- **Empowerment of Courts**: It empowers the Supreme Court to issue various writs to protect fundamental rights, ensuring judicial oversight and protection.
- **Supremacy of the Constitution**: By guaranteeing the right to constitutional remedies, Article 32 reinforces the supremacy of the Constitution and the rule of law.

Types of Writs under Article 32

The Supreme Court has the power to issue five types of writs for the enforcement of fundamental rights:

1. **Habeas Corpus**: A writ used to secure the release of a person unlawfully detained or imprisoned. It protects individual liberty by ensuring that no person is deprived of their freedom without due process of law.

2. **Mandamus**: A writ issued to compel a public authority to perform a duty that it has failed to fulfill. It ensures that public officials and bodies act within their legal bounds.
3. **Prohibition**: A writ issued to prohibit a lower court or tribunal from exceeding its jurisdiction or acting contrary to the law. It is a preventive measure.
4. **Certiorari**: A writ issued to quash the order or decision of a lower court or tribunal that exceeds its jurisdiction or contains an error of law. It ensures judicial review and correction of legal errors.
5. **Quo Warranto**: A writ issued to challenge the legality of a person's claim to a public office. It ensures that only legally qualified individuals occupy public positions.

Significance of the Right to Constitutional Remedies

The right to constitutional remedies is vital for several reasons:

1. **Enforcement of Fundamental Rights**: It provides a mechanism to enforce fundamental rights, ensuring that they are not merely theoretical but practical and actionable.
2. **Judicial Oversight**: It empowers the judiciary to protect individuals' rights and to review the actions of the executive and legislative branches, maintaining a system of checks and balances.
3. **Protection of Rule of Law**: It reinforces the rule of law by ensuring that all actions by public authorities are subject to judicial scrutiny.
4. **Safeguard against Arbitrary Actions**: It protects individuals from arbitrary actions by public authorities, ensuring accountability and transparency in governance.

Judicial Interpretation and Landmark Cases

The judiciary has played a pivotal role in interpreting and expanding the scope of the right to constitutional remedies. Some landmark judgments include:

1. **Romesh Thappar v. State of Madras (1950)**: The Supreme Court held that freedom of speech and expression was violated and emphasized the importance of Article 32 in protecting fundamental rights.
2. **Maneka Gandhi v. Union of India (1978)**: The Court expanded the interpretation of Article 21 (Right to Life and Personal Liberty) and reinforced the importance of Article 32 in ensuring the protection of fundamental rights.
3. **Bandhua Mukti Morcha v. Union of India (1984)**: The Court used Article 32 to address the issue of bonded labor, illustrating its role in upholding social justice.
4. **Vineet Narain v. Union of India (1998)**: The Court issued directions to ensure the independence of investigative agencies, demonstrating the use of Article 32 to ensure accountability in governance.

Comparative Perspective

Comparing the right to constitutional remedies in India with similar provisions in other constitutions, such as the United States Constitution (which provides for judicial review) and the European Convention on Human Rights (which allows individuals to bring cases before the European Court of Human Rights), highlights both similarities and unique features:

- **United States**: The U.S. Constitution does not explicitly provide for writs, but the judiciary has developed similar remedies through judicial review.
- **European Convention on Human Rights**: The Convention provides for individual applications to the European Court of Human Rights, offering a supranational mechanism for the enforcement of human rights.

Challenges and Contemporary Issues

Despite constitutional guarantees, several challenges persist in fully realizing the right to constitutional remedies:

1. **Access to Justice**: Ensuring that all individuals, especially those from marginalized communities, have access to the Supreme Court for the enforcement of their rights remains a significant challenge.
2. **Judicial Overload**: The Supreme Court is often burdened with a high volume of cases, which can lead to delays in the enforcement of fundamental rights.
3. **Awareness and Legal Literacy**: Increasing public awareness and legal literacy about constitutional remedies is essential to empower citizens to seek judicial protection of their rights.
4. **Balancing Judicial Activism and Restraint**: The judiciary must balance its role in protecting fundamental rights with the need to respect the separation of powers and avoid overstepping its jurisdiction.

Conclusion

The right to constitutional remedies is fundamental to the Indian Constitution's vision of a democratic and just society.

Understanding the scope, significance, and judicial interpretation of Article 32 is crucial for students of constitutional law. As future legal practitioners and scholars, it is essential to recognize the role of this right in safeguarding individual liberties, promoting social justice, and ensuring the rule of law in India.

CHAPTER-IV(i)

Directive Principles of State Policy

The Constitution of India, adopted in 1950, is not just a legal document but a vision for a democratic and inclusive society. While the Fundamental Rights provide a framework for individual liberties, the Directive Principles of State Policy (DPSP) outlined in Part IV of the Constitution serve as guiding principles for the state to promote social and economic welfare. This chapter delves into the origins, objectives, nature, and significance of the Directive Principles, exploring their role in shaping the policies and laws in India.

Historical Background and Philosophical Foundation

The concept of Directive Principles has its roots in the Irish Constitution, from which it was borrowed. The framers of the Indian Constitution, influenced by various social and economic theories, sought to incorporate principles that would help in the establishment of a welfare state. The Directive Principles reflect the ideals and aspirations of the people of India, aiming to bridge the gap between the rich and the poor, and ensure social and economic justice.

Objectives of Directive Principles

The primary objectives of the Directive Principles are:

1. **Promoting Welfare of the People (Article 38)**: To secure a social order for the promotion of welfare of the people by striving to minimize inequalities in income and

eliminate inequalities in status, facilities, and opportunities.
2. **Achieving Economic Justice (Articles 39-39A)**: Ensuring that the ownership and control of material resources are distributed to serve the common good, preventing the concentration of wealth, and promoting equal pay for equal work for both men and women.
3. **Social Justice (Articles 41-43A)**: Making provisions for securing the right to work, education, and public assistance in cases of unemployment, old age, sickness, and disablement. Promoting the participation of workers in the management of industries.
4. **Environmental Protection (Article 48A)**: Directing the state to protect and improve the environment and safeguard forests and wildlife.
5. **Promotion of Education and Public Health (Articles 45-47)**: Emphasizing the provision of free and compulsory education for children, raising the level of nutrition, and improving public health.

Key Provisions of the Directive Principles

The Directive Principles are broadly classified into various categories based on their objectives:

1. **Social and Economic Rights**
    - **Article 38**: State to secure a social order for the promotion of welfare of the people.
    - **Article 39**: Certain principles of policy to be followed by the State, including the distribution of wealth, prevention of exploitation, and equal pay for equal work.

- **Article 39A**: Provision of free legal aid and ensuring that justice is not denied to any citizen due to economic or other disabilities.
- **Article 41**: Right to work, education, and public assistance in certain cases.

2. **Directive for Social Welfare**
   - **Article 42**: Provision for just and humane conditions of work and maternity relief.
   - **Article 43**: Living wage for workers.
   - **Article 43A**: Participation of workers in management of industries.

3. **Education and Cultural Rights**
   - **Article 45**: Provision for free and compulsory education for children.
   - **Article 46**: Promotion of educational and economic interests of Scheduled Castes, Scheduled Tribes, and other weaker sections.

4. **Health and Nutrition**
   - **Article 47**: Duty of the State to raise the level of nutrition and standard of living and to improve public health.

5. **Environmental Protection**
   - **Article 48**: Organisation of agriculture and animal husbandry.
   - **Article 48A**: Protection and improvement of environment and safeguarding of forests and wildlife.

6. **Promotion of International Peace and Security**
   - **Article 51**: Promotion of international peace and security, maintenance of just and honorable relations between nations, fostering respect for international law and treaty

obligations, and encouraging settlement of international disputes by arbitration.

Nature and Significance

The Directive Principles are non-justiciable, meaning they are not enforceable by any court. However, they are fundamental in the governance of the country and aim to create a social framework for the economic and social well-being of the people. Their significance lies in:

1. **Guiding Legislative and Executive Actions**: They serve as guidelines for the central and state governments in framing laws and policies.
2. **Reflecting Social and Economic Goals**: They outline the goals that the state should strive to achieve, such as reducing inequality, promoting education, and improving health.
3. **Influencing Judicial Decisions**: Although non-justiciable, the courts have often referred to the Directive Principles in their judgments to interpret Fundamental Rights and other constitutional provisions.

Implementation and Challenges

Over the years, various governments have taken steps to implement the Directive Principles through legislation and policy measures. Some notable examples include:

- **Land Reforms**: Redistributing land to reduce inequality and prevent concentration of land ownership.
- **Employment Guarantee Schemes**: Initiatives like the Mahatma Gandhi National Rural Employment

Guarantee Act (MGNREGA) aim to provide employment and enhance livelihood security in rural areas.
- **Education and Health Programs**: The implementation of the Right to Education Act and various health schemes to improve public health and education standards.

However, challenges remain in fully realizing the objectives of the Directive Principles. These challenges include:

1. **Resource Constraints**: Implementing welfare measures requires substantial financial resources, which can be a constraint for the government.
2. **Political Will**: Achieving the goals set out in the Directive Principles requires strong political will and commitment from the government.
3. **Balancing Fundamental Rights and Directive Principles**: Ensuring that the implementation of Directive Principles does not infringe upon Fundamental Rights.

Judicial Interpretation and Evolution

The judiciary has played a crucial role in interpreting and evolving the relationship between Fundamental Rights and Directive Principles. Some landmark judgments include:

1. **Champakam Dorairajan Case (1951)**: The Supreme Court held that Fundamental Rights would prevail over Directive Principles in case of a conflict.
2. **Golak Nath Case (1967)**: Reiterated the supremacy of Fundamental Rights over Directive Principles.
3. **Kesavananda Bharati Case (1973)**: Introduced the basic structure doctrine and emphasized the harmony

and balance between Fundamental Rights and Directive Principles.
4. **Minerva Mills Case (1980)**: Reinforced the idea that Fundamental Rights and Directive Principles are complementary and that a balance must be maintained between them.

Conclusion

The Directive Principles of State Policy are a testament to the vision of the framers of the Indian Constitution, aiming to establish a just and equitable society. While they are not enforceable by law, their significance lies in guiding the state towards achieving social and economic justice. For students of constitutional law, understanding the Directive Principles is crucial to appreciating the broader goals and aspirations of the Indian Constitution. The interplay between Directive Principles and Fundamental Rights reflects the dynamic and evolving nature of constitutional governance in India, striving to balance individual freedoms with social welfare.

CHAPTER-IV(ii)

The Relationship between Directive Principles of State Policy and Fundamental Rights

Introduction

The Constitution of India, adopted in 1950, is a comprehensive document that seeks to balance individual liberties with the socio-economic goals of the state. Part III of the Constitution enumerates the Fundamental Rights, which are enforceable by the courts and guarantee individual freedoms. Part IV, on the other hand, contains the Directive Principles of State Policy (DPSP), which are non-justiciable guidelines for the state to promote social and economic welfare. This chapter explores the intricate relationship between these two parts, highlighting their complementarities, conflicts, and the role of judicial interpretation in harmonizing them.

Fundamental Rights: An Overview

Fundamental Rights, enshrined in Articles 12 to 35 of Part III, provide a framework for individual freedoms and civil liberties. These rights are justiciable, meaning that individuals can approach the courts for their enforcement. Key Fundamental Rights include:

- **Right to Equality (Articles 14-18)**: Ensures equality before the law and prohibits discrimination.

- **Right to Freedom (Articles 19-22)**: Covers various freedoms such as speech, assembly, and movement.
- **Right Against Exploitation (Articles 23-24)**: Prohibits human trafficking and child labor.
- **Right to Freedom of Religion (Articles 25-28)**: Secures religious freedom.
- **Cultural and Educational Rights (Articles 29-30)**: Protects the rights of minorities.
- **Right to Constitutional Remedies (Article 32)**: Allows individuals to seek enforcement of Fundamental Rights through the courts.

Directive Principles of State Policy: An Overview

Directive Principles, outlined in Articles 36 to 51 of Part IV, are guidelines for the state to ensure social and economic democracy. Although not enforceable by courts, these principles are fundamental in the governance of the country. Key Directive Principles include:

- **Article 38**: Promotes the welfare of the people by securing a social order with justice.
- **Article 39**: Ensures that wealth is not concentrated and resources are distributed for the common good.
- **Article 41**: Right to work, education, and public assistance.
- **Article 43**: Living wage and decent conditions of work.
- **Article 45**: Free and compulsory education for children.
- **Article 47**: Raising the level of nutrition and improving public health.
- **Article 48A**: Protection of the environment.

Complementary Nature

Fundamental Rights and Directive Principles are designed to complement each other. Fundamental Rights provide the basic conditions for the exercise of individual liberties, while Directive Principles aim to create a socio-economic framework that supports these liberties. Together, they form the core of the Constitution's vision for a democratic and equitable society.

For example, the Right to Education Act (2009) stems from both the Fundamental Right to Education (Article 21A) and the Directive Principle under Article 45, which emphasizes free and compulsory education for children. Similarly, the principles of equality and non-discrimination under Fundamental Rights are reinforced by the Directive Principles' focus on social and economic justice.

Conflict and Judicial Interpretation

Despite their complementary nature, there have been instances where Directive Principles and Fundamental Rights have come into conflict. The judiciary has played a crucial role in resolving these conflicts and harmonizing the two sets of provisions.

Champakam Dorairajan Case (1951) In this case, the Supreme Court held that Fundamental Rights would prevail over Directive Principles in case of a conflict. This decision underscored the enforceability of Fundamental Rights over the non-justiciable Directive Principles.

Golak Nath Case (1967) The Supreme Court reiterated the supremacy of Fundamental Rights over Directive Principles, stating that Parliament could not amend Fundamental Rights to implement Directive Principles.

Kesavananda Bharati Case (1973) This landmark case introduced the basic structure doctrine, asserting that while Parliament has the power to amend the Constitution, it cannot alter the basic structure, which includes the harmony and balance between Fundamental Rights and Directive Principles. The Court emphasized that both are integral to the Constitution and should be read harmoniously.

Minerva Mills Case (1980) The Supreme Court reinforced the idea that Fundamental Rights and Directive Principles are complementary, stating that a balance must be maintained between them. The Court invalidated amendments that sought to give absolute primacy to Directive Principles over Fundamental Rights, reiterating the importance of both sets of provisions in achieving the constitutional vision.

Reconciliatory Approach

The judiciary has often adopted a reconciliatory approach to interpret Fundamental Rights and Directive Principles in a manner that upholds the spirit of the Constitution. By doing so, the courts have ensured that the implementation of Directive Principles does not infringe upon Fundamental Rights. This approach is evident in several judgments where the courts have referred to Directive Principles to interpret the scope and ambit of Fundamental Rights.

For example, in the **Unni Krishnan Case (1993)**, the Supreme Court read the right to education into the right to life under Article 21, drawing inspiration from Article 45 of the Directive Principles. Similarly, in the **Olga Tellis Case (1985)**, the Court held that the right to livelihood is an integral part of the right to life, drawing from the Directive Principles.

Implementation and Legislative Measures

Over the years, various legislative measures have been taken to implement the Directive Principles, often aligning them with Fundamental Rights. Some notable examples include:

- **Land Reforms**: Redistributing land to reduce inequality and prevent the concentration of land ownership, inspired by Articles 38 and 39.
- **Employment Guarantee Schemes**: Initiatives like the Mahatma Gandhi National Rural Employment Guarantee Act (MGNREGA) aim to provide employment and enhance livelihood security in rural areas, reflecting Article 41.
- **Right to Information Act (2005)**: Promotes transparency and accountability in governance, aligning with Article 38.

These measures demonstrate the state's commitment to achieving the socio-economic goals outlined in the Directive Principles while respecting the Fundamental Rights of individuals.

Comparative Chart: **Similarities and Differences between Directive Principles of State Policy and Fundamental Rights**

Aspect	Fundamental Rights	Directive Principles of State Policy

Location in the Constitution	Part III (Articles 12-35)	Part IV (Articles 36-51)
Enforceability	Justiciable and enforceable by courts	Non-justiciable and not enforceable by courts
Nature	Negative obligations on the state	Positive obligations on the state
Objective	Protect individual liberties and rights	Promote social and economic welfare
Scope	Civil and political rights	Socio-economic rights and principles
Examples	Right to Equality, Right to Freedom, Right to Constitutional Remedies	Right to Work, Right to Education, Promotion of Welfare of People
Judicial Interpretation	Can be directly enforced by the judiciary	Can guide judicial interpretation but not enforceable
Amendability	Subject to judicial review; part of the basic structure doctrine (post	Can be amended by Parliament, provided it does not infringe upon

	Kesavananda Bharati case)	the basic structure of the Constitution
Influence on Legislation	Directly influences and restricts legislative actions	Guides the state in making laws and policies
Conflict Resolution	Fundamental Rights generally prevail in case of conflict (post Champakam Dorairajan case)	Must be harmonized with Fundamental Rights (post Kesavananda Bharati and Minerva Mills cases)
Examples of Implementation	Laws upholding freedom of speech, right to information, right to privacy	Laws on land reforms, employment guarantees, free and compulsory education
Philosophical Foundation	Liberal democratic tradition emphasizing individual freedoms	Socialistic and welfare-oriented goals emphasizing community and social justice
International Influence	Inspired by Bill of Rights, Universal Declaration of Human Rights	Inspired by Irish Constitution and socio-economic goals of welfare states

Explanation of the Comparative Chart

- **Location in the Constitution**: Fundamental Rights are found in Part III, while Directive Principles are in Part IV.
- **Enforceability**: Fundamental Rights are enforceable by courts, allowing individuals to seek judicial remedies. Directive Principles are non-justiciable, meaning they cannot be enforced by courts.
- **Nature**: Fundamental Rights often impose negative obligations, requiring the state to refrain from certain actions. Directive Principles impose positive obligations, requiring the state to take specific actions to promote social welfare.
- **Objective**: Fundamental Rights aim to protect individual liberties and personal freedoms, while Directive Principles aim to promote social and economic welfare for the collective good.
- **Scope**: Fundamental Rights cover civil and political rights, whereas Directive Principles cover socio-economic rights and state policy guidelines.
- **Examples**: Fundamental Rights include the Right to Equality and the Right to Freedom. Directive Principles include the Right to Work and the Promotion of Welfare of People.
- **Judicial Interpretation**: Fundamental Rights can be directly enforced and interpreted by the judiciary. Directive Principles, while non-justiciable, can guide judicial interpretation in some cases.
- **Amenability**: Fundamental Rights are subject to judicial review and are considered part of the basic structure of the Constitution. Directive Principles can be amended by Parliament, provided such amendments do not alter the Constitution's basic structure.

- **Influence on Legislation**: Fundamental Rights restrict legislative actions that infringe on individual liberties. Directive Principles guide the state in formulating laws and policies aimed at social and economic welfare.
- **Conflict Resolution**: In cases of conflict, Fundamental Rights generally prevail, but the judiciary strives to harmonize both sets of provisions to uphold the Constitution's overall vision.
- **Examples of Implementation**: Fundamental Rights have led to laws protecting freedom of speech, right to information, and privacy. Directive Principles have inspired laws on land reforms, employment guarantees, and free education.
- **Philosophical Foundation**: Fundamental Rights are rooted in liberal democratic traditions that emphasize individual freedoms. Directive Principles are influenced by socialistic and welfare-oriented goals aimed at achieving social justice.
- **International Influence**: Fundamental Rights draw inspiration from documents like the Bill of Rights and the Universal Declaration of Human Rights. Directive Principles are influenced by the Irish Constitution and the socio-economic goals of welfare states.

This comparative chart and explanation provide a comprehensive overview of the similarities and differences between Directive Principles of State Policy and Fundamental Rights, highlighting their distinct yet complementary roles in the Indian Constitution.

Conclusion

The relationship between Directive Principles of State Policy and Fundamental Rights is complex yet complementary. While Fundamental Rights provide a framework for individual liberties,

Directive Principles guide the state towards creating a just and equitable society. The judiciary has played a crucial role in harmonizing these provisions, ensuring that the Constitution's vision of a balanced and inclusive democracy is realized. For students, understanding this relationship is key to appreciating the dynamic nature of the Indian Constitution and its commitment to both individual freedom and social welfare.

CHAPTER-V

Fundamental Duties under the Constitution of India

Introduction

The Constitution of India, a living document that guides the largest democracy in the world, not only enumerates the rights and freedoms of its citizens but also emphasizes their responsibilities. Fundamental Duties, enshrined in Part IV-A of the Constitution, underscore the importance of responsible citizenship in promoting the collective well-being of the nation. This chapter explores the genesis, significance, and scope of Fundamental Duties, providing students with a comprehensive understanding of their role in the constitutional framework.

Historical Background

Fundamental Duties were not originally part of the Constitution when it was adopted in 1950. They were introduced through the 42nd Amendment Act of 1976, inspired by the constitutions of socialist countries, particularly the former Soviet Union. The 42nd Amendment Act of 1976 added a new chapter to the Constitution, Part IVA, which lists ten Fundamental Duties. This inclusion was aimed at emphasizing that while citizens enjoy certain rights, they also have corresponding duties towards the nation and society.

Swaran Singh Committee

The Swaran Singh Committee, appointed by the government in 1976, recommended the inclusion of Fundamental Duties in the Constitution. The committee believed that duties were essential to balance the extensive Fundamental Rights enjoyed by citizens. The committee's recommendations led to the insertion of Article 51A, which initially listed ten duties. An eleventh duty was added by the 86th Amendment in 2002.

Nature and Scope

Unlike Fundamental Rights, Fundamental Duties are non-justiciable, meaning they are not enforceable by law. However, they carry moral and ethical significance, guiding citizens' behavior and actions. The inclusion of Fundamental Duties is intended to remind citizens that while they enjoy rights and freedoms, they also have responsibilities towards the nation and society.

Significance of Fundamental Duties

Fundamental Duties serve several important purposes in the Indian constitutional framework:

1. **Reinforcing National Unity**: By emphasizing respect for national symbols and the integrity of the nation, Fundamental Duties foster a sense of unity and patriotism.

2. **Promoting Social Harmony**: Duties such as promoting harmony and renouncing practices derogatory to women encourage social cohesion and respect for diversity.
3. **Environmental Protection**: Duties related to protecting the environment highlight the citizens' role in sustainable development.
4. **Encouraging Civic Responsibility**: By stressing the importance of safeguarding public property and maintaining peace, Fundamental Duties promote responsible citizenship.
5. **Fostering Educational and Scientific Development**: The duty to develop scientific temper and ensure educational opportunities underscores the importance of intellectual growth and informed citizenship.

List of Fundamental Duties

Article 51A outlines the Fundamental Duties of every citizen of India. These duties are:

1. **To abide by the Constitution and respect its ideals and institutions, the National Flag, and the National Anthem.**
2. **To cherish and follow the noble ideals which inspired our national struggle for freedom.**
3. **To uphold and protect the sovereignty, unity, and integrity of India.**
4. **To defend the country and render national service when called upon to do so.**
5. **To promote harmony and the spirit of common brotherhood amongst all the people of India, transcending religious, linguistic, and regional or

sectional diversities; to renounce practices derogatory to the dignity of women.
6. To value and preserve the rich heritage of our composite culture.
7. To protect and improve the natural environment including forests, lakes, rivers, and wildlife, and to have compassion for living creatures.
8. To develop the scientific temper, humanism, and the spirit of inquiry and reform.
9. To safeguard public property and to abjure violence.
10. To strive towards excellence in all spheres of individual and collective activity so that the nation constantly rises to higher levels of endeavor and achievement.
11. To provide opportunities for education to children between the ages of 6 and 14 years, a duty added by the 86th Amendment Act.

Analysing Fundamental Duties

(a) To Abide by the Constitution and Respect its Ideals and Institutions, the National Flag and the National Anthem

This duty emphasizes the importance of upholding the Constitution and its principles. Respecting the Constitution means acknowledging its supremacy and adhering to its provisions in all aspects of life. This includes respecting the National Flag and the National Anthem, symbols of the nation's sovereignty and unity.

Understanding this duty underscores the significance of constitutional literacy. Understanding the Constitution's ideals and institutions is fundamental to appreciating the rule of law, democracy, and the rights and responsibilities that come with citizenship. Celebrating national symbols fosters a sense of national identity and pride.

(b) To Cherish and Follow the Noble Ideals Which Inspired Our National Struggle for Freedom

The duty to cherish and follow the ideals of the freedom struggle highlights the importance of remembering and honoring the sacrifices made by freedom fighters. It emphasizes the values of justice, liberty, equality, and fraternity that guided the independence movement.

This duty encourages the study of history and the freedom struggle. It fosters an understanding of the principles that shaped modern India and inspires a commitment to uphold these values in contemporary society.

(c) To Uphold and Protect the Sovereignty, Unity, and Integrity of India

This duty underscores the importance of maintaining the nation's sovereignty, unity, and territorial integrity. It calls for loyalty to the country and a commitment to national solidarity.

This duty emphasizes the significance of national security and the need to stand united against threats to the nation's sovereignty. It encourages a sense of patriotism and the importance of working together to preserve national unity.

(d) To Defend the Country and Render National Service When Called Upon to Do So

This duty highlights the responsibility to defend the nation against external and internal threats. It includes serving in the armed forces or other national services when required.

This duty underscores the importance of being prepared to serve the nation in times of need. It fosters a spirit of readiness and willingness to contribute to national defense and public service.

(e) To Promote Harmony and the Spirit of Common Brotherhood amongst All the People of India Transcending Religious, Linguistic, and Regional or Sectional Diversities; To Renounce Practices Derogatory to the Dignity of Women

This duty emphasizes the importance of promoting social harmony and unity among diverse groups. It calls for transcending religious, linguistic, and regional differences to foster a sense of common brotherhood. It also includes renouncing practices that undermine the dignity of women.

This duty highlights the importance of tolerance, inclusivity, and gender equality. It encourages efforts to bridge social divides and promote mutual respect and understanding.

(f) To Value and Preserve the Rich Heritage of Our Composite Culture

This duty underscores the importance of valuing and preserving India's rich cultural heritage. It calls for respect and preservation of the diverse cultural traditions that make up the nation's composite culture.

This duty emphasizes the significance of cultural awareness and heritage conservation. It encourages appreciation of the nation's cultural diversity and efforts to preserve and promote cultural traditions.

(g) To Protect and Improve the Natural Environment Including Forests, Lakes, Rivers, and Wildlife, and to Have Compassion for Living Creatures

This duty highlights the responsibility to protect and improve the natural environment. It calls for efforts to conserve forests, water bodies, and wildlife and to show compassion towards all living creatures.

This duty emphasizes the importance of environmental conservation and sustainable living. It encourages actions to protect natural resources and promote ecological balance.

(h) To Develop the Scientific Temper, Humanism, and the Spirit of Inquiry and Reform

This duty underscores the importance of developing a scientific temper, humanism, and a spirit of inquiry and reform. It calls for rational thinking, curiosity, and a commitment to social progress.

This duty emphasizes the value of education, critical thinking, and innovation. It encourages a lifelong pursuit of knowledge and a commitment to improving society through informed and rational actions.

(i) To Safeguard Public Property and to Abjure Violence

This duty highlights the responsibility to protect public property and refrain from violence. It calls for respect for public assets and a commitment to non-violence in all actions.

This duty emphasizes the importance of civic responsibility and respect for community resources. It encourages peaceful and constructive ways of addressing conflicts and contributing to the common good.

(j) To Strive Towards Excellence in All Spheres of Individual and Collective Activity So That the Nation Constantly Rises to Higher Levels of Endeavor and Achievement

This duty underscores the importance of striving for excellence in all endeavors. It calls for continuous improvement and efforts to achieve higher standards in personal and collective activities.

This duty emphasizes the value of hard work, dedication, and a commitment to excellence. It encourages a pursuit of academic, professional, and personal growth to contribute to the nation's progress.

(k) Who is a Parent or Guardian to Provide Opportunities for Education to His Child or, as the Case May Be, Ward Between the Age of Six and Fourteen Years

This duty highlights the responsibility of parents and guardians to provide educational opportunities for their children. It emphasizes the importance of ensuring that children receive education during their formative years.

This duty underscores the significance of education as a fundamental right and a crucial factor in personal and national development. It encourages a commitment to learning and the importance of supporting educational opportunities for all.

Importance of Fundamental Duties

Complementing Fundamental Rights

Fundamental Duties serve as a balance to Fundamental Rights, reminding citizens that rights come with corresponding responsibilities. While Fundamental Rights empower individuals, Fundamental Duties emphasize their role in ensuring the collective well-being of society.

Promoting Civic Responsibility

These duties inculcate a sense of civic responsibility and national pride among citizens. They encourage individuals to act in ways that contribute to the nation's development and uphold its democratic values. Understanding and internalizing these duties fosters responsible behavior and active participation in nation-building.

Enhancing Social Cohesion

Fundamental Duties promote social harmony and unity. By encouraging citizens to transcend religious, linguistic, and regional diversities, these duties help in building a cohesive and inclusive society. They emphasize the importance of unity in diversity, a cornerstone of India's pluralistic society.

Protecting the Environment

One of the Fundamental Duties emphasizes the protection and improvement of the natural environment. This duty highlights the importance of environmental conservation, teaching the value of sustainable living and the need to protect natural resources for future generations.

Encouraging Scientific Temper

The duty to develop a scientific temper and humanism underscores the importance of rational thinking, inquiry, and innovation. This duty encourages a spirit of curiosity, critical thinking, and the pursuit of knowledge, essential for personal and national progress.

Fundamental Duties and Education

Role in Curriculum

Incorporating Fundamental Duties into the educational curriculum is essential for raising awareness among citizens. Schools and colleges can play a pivotal role in teaching these duties through civics education, encouraging individuals to understand and practice their civic responsibilities.

Practical Implementation

Educational institutions can promote Fundamental Duties through various activities such as debates, discussions, and community service projects. For example, organizing cleanliness drives, tree planting campaigns, and cultural programs can help individuals actively participate in fulfilling their duties towards the environment and society.

Encouraging Critical Thinking

Teaching Fundamental Duties should not be limited to rote learning. Educators should encourage citizens to critically analyze these duties and understand their relevance in contemporary society. Discussions on real-life applications and challenges related to these duties can foster deeper understanding and engagement.

Role of Education and Media

Education and media play a crucial role in promoting awareness and understanding of Fundamental Duties. Educational curricula should include lessons on Fundamental Duties to instill a sense of responsibility among students from a young age. Media campaigns can also highlight the importance of these duties, encouraging citizens to actively participate in nation-building.

Judicial Interpretation and Enforcement

Non-Justiciable Nature

Unlike Fundamental Rights, Fundamental Duties are non-justiciable, meaning they cannot be enforced by the courts. However, their importance is acknowledged in various judicial pronouncements, where courts have emphasized the need to uphold these duties for the larger good of society.

Judicial References

In several cases, the judiciary has highlighted the significance of Fundamental Duties. For instance, in the case of *Ranganath Mishra vs. Union of India* (1992), the Supreme Court observed that while Fundamental Duties are not enforceable by law, they provide valuable guidance for judicial interpretation of constitutional and legal provisions.

Legislative Measures

Though non-justiciable, the government has enacted various laws that indirectly enforce Fundamental Duties. For example, laws related to environmental protection, preservation of cultural heritage, and prohibition of violence reflect the duties outlined in Article 51A.

While Fundamental Duties are non-justiciable, the judiciary has occasionally referred to them in its judgments to emphasize the importance of responsible citizenship. For instance:

- **In the case of *AIIMS Students Union v. AIIMS* (2001), the Supreme Court highlighted the duty to develop a scientific temper and spirit of inquiry.**
- **In *M.C. Mehta v. Union of India* (1988), the Supreme Court invoked the duty to protect the environment, emphasizing citizens' role in environmental conservation.**

These references illustrate how Fundamental Duties, despite their non-justiciable nature, influence the judicial understanding of citizens' responsibilities.

Comparative Perspective

Fundamental Duties in India can be compared with similar provisions in other countries. For example:

- **The Constitution of Japan includes duties related to education and work.**
- **The German Basic Law emphasizes the duty to protect the natural foundations of life.**
- **The Constitution of Russia outlines duties such as paying taxes and preserving cultural heritage.**

These comparisons highlight that the concept of duties as complementary to rights is not unique to India but is a common feature in many constitutional democracies.

Challenges in Implementation

Despite their importance, the implementation of Fundamental Duties faces several challenges:

1. **Lack of Awareness**: Many citizens are unaware of the Fundamental Duties and their significance.
2. **Absence of Legal Enforcement**: Being non-justiciable, there is no legal mechanism to enforce Fundamental Duties, relying instead on moral and ethical persuasion.
3. **Cultural and Social Barriers**: Deep-rooted cultural practices and social norms can sometimes hinder the effective realization of duties, such as promoting gender equality and protecting the environment.

Conclusion

Fundamental Duties, though non-justiciable, form an integral part of the Indian Constitution. They remind citizens that while they enjoy various rights, they also have corresponding responsibilities towards the nation and society. Understanding and embracing these duties is crucial for the holistic development of individuals and the nation. For students, a comprehensive grasp of Fundamental Duties complements their knowledge of Fundamental Rights, fostering a balanced perspective on their roles and responsibilities as citizens of India.

www.ingramcontent.com/pod-product-compliance
Lightning Source LLC
Chambersburg PA
CBHW071833210526
45479CB00001B/118